# Paradig

'It is amazing how God can take a rationalist atheist and transform him into a passionate evangelist using the scientist's own assessment methodology. Roy's professional credentials show him to be a man of deep intellect and scientific integrity, and *Paradigm Shift* shows how all of this can be brought together and enhanced by faith in the Lord Jesus Christ. A powerful encouragement for all who think science and faith are difficult bedfellows. This is the story of a man whose life I covet.'

**Revd Paul Springate – Director of the Harnhill Centre for Christian Healing**

'Roy Peacock works in a world where the laws of physics and formulae are used to prove or disprove theories: if it can't be proved then it (probably) doesn't exist! In *Paradigm Shift* he shares some of the 'unbelievable' but real events that have happened during his life – events that have shaped it and where some of those basic scientific laws have themselves been challenged. Here the scientist, employing all the skills and expertise used in his scientific world, proves his personal and tangible knowledge of a living Christ, taking such things above intellect and learning, but using intellect and learning as his guidelines.

'Roy skilfully and simply opens up the realities of the journey he has been on and the remarkable interventions of God that have brought about the paradigm shift in his understanding of the relevance of God to us all.'

**Geoff Booker – former publisher and founder of the Quicken Trust**

'When the radiant face of his wife prompted tentative steps into a world he considered to be well outside the realm of science, Roy's journey resulted in the unexpected discovery that the source of her new-found joy was also the source of the laws operating within his scientific framework.

'For those in search of meaning, and those who have found meaning but struggle to put it altogether, the insights provided in this book will be as pearls of great price.'

*Professor Keith Cleland – Professor and Head, Financial Management, IBR School of Executive Management, Steinbeis University, Berlin*

'Roy Peacock has written a remarkable book. In my many years of seeking to walk with the Lord, I have never before been presented with such a clear, compelling and faith-building understanding of God's amazing consistency! As Creator, God must know all about thermodynamics, the study and application of which lies at the heart of the author's calling. How many times have I heard tell of a conflict between science and faith – between the rational and the irrational! Here we have a definitive writing from one who knows and has experience in both scientific and spiritual environments.

'Having known Roy for nearly thirty years, I am aware that he has had to omit many other significant works with which he has been associated. Allow me to take the opportunity to record my deep gratitude for his support in developing the 'Transformed Working Life' teaching in the early years of the International Christian Chamber of Commerce in this country, and our partnership in launching Carpenter's

Trust through which teaching and discipling was a central feature.

'I trust that this excellent book will be widely read and that, through it, God will be honoured and his servant rightly encouraged.'

*Michael Fenton-Jones – company chairman, past President of the International Christian Chamber of Commerce*

'The two laws of the kingdom of God – to love God with all our heart, mind and strength and to love our neighbour as ourselves – are as inviolate as the two laws of thermodynamics; by keeping them and following them all the other principles and laws of his kingdom (super)naturally follow.

'At no point are followers of Jesus of Nazareth promised trouble-free lives, but as Roy and Elizabeth can testify, no matter how deep the despair or how high the joy, Jesus has always been with them.

'I have known Roy for almost thirty years and every time that I have heard him or read him, I have invariably had my mind stretched and challenged and my spirit inspired, and my whole being has yearned for something more. This beautifully argued, easy-to-read personal life story is no exception.'

*Anthony Cordle – businessman, politician, former soldier, follower of Jesus Christ*

'As a very successful scientist, Roy struggled to reconcile his well-trained thought processes with the active presence of the Lord Jesus in his life. His story carries the reader along with him on his exciting journey. I have known Roy over many years, well enough to recognize that he always speaks the truth and has usually thought through the subject carefully before speaking. When he asked me to look at his new book, he said, 'Just read the first and last chapter and possibly the Postscript as that will give you an idea of what I am trying to say.' Poor advice – once I started reading I was quite unable to stop. An inspiring read.'

**David Wells, FRCGP – physician and trustee of the Harnhill Centre for Christian Healing**

'Professor Roy Peacock's *Paradigm Shift* offers a highly stimulating memoir of a scientist's journey from questioning scepticism to faith and commitment to Jesus Christ. In vivid terms he describes the decisive point of his conversion: "It was as if a tectonic plate upon which my life was founded had taken a massive shift." There was to be no turning back. Skilfully he illustrates, from his work in the aerospace industry and from many other experiences along the way, how the truth, love and power of God transforms human lives and situations. This is a welcome faith-raiser to challenge and encourage the reader, and to pass on to others.

'A timely book, too, from a gifted communicator, for lively and fruitful discussion!'

**Right Revd John Perry – former Bishop of Chelmsford**

'The experience of death at an aeroplane crash deepened Roy's scientific purpose. The death, long ago, of a carpenter's son moved the tectonic plates of Roy's life even further, to perceive reality for the first time. So a clever scientist tasted his own death to discover that the rubbish heap of life could become, with God, a beautiful garden. Roy shows that humility is the only way to know God. This book has the key to release successful, talented people from their ego so as to escape into a glorious future.'

*John Wright – evangelist and banker;*
*founder of two private banks.*

'Roy tells his personal, inspiring and challenging story of life in a supernatural dimension. He demonstrates that science and faith can walk together. I read Paradigm Shift in one session totally absorbed by the challenges and miracles he has experienced. Written with pace, passion, honesty and humour, this account of the life of a scientist, prophetic teacher and healing evangelist will build your faith.'

*Don Latham – accountant, former Chief Executive,*
*West Wiltshire District Council,*
*public sector consultant, motivational speaker.*

'The belief that science and faith are incompatible has become so deeply cemented in the modern mind that it has become one of the primary reasons people give for rejecting the possibility that faith might offer anything of value or relevance to their lives. *Paradigm Shift* offers a convincing antidote to this belief, as Roy uses his own story, rich in both scientific and spiritual experience, to explore the broader story of the times in which we live, examining our inner landscape of doubt, agnosticism, atheism and faith. Throughout, he offers a number of insights into the love, commitment and labour which has nurtured his own marriage. This timely book will be welcomed by all who wish to explore the enticing possibility of a similarly strong and harmonious relationship between science and faith.'

*Revd Paul Langham – Vicar of Christ Church, Clifton, Bristol*

ROY PEACOCK was born in Bristol in England. He studied as a post-graduate student pursuing research at the Cranfield Institute of Technology and the University of Cambridge, and worked in industry for Bristol Aero Engines, Bristol-Siddeley Engines and Rolls-Royce. In 1994 he founded Thermodyne, a specialist company that has provided engineering design solutions for a range of companies in the UK, USA and Italy. He has accumulated wide experience acting as a consultant or advisor to government departments and agencies in the UK, USA, India and elsewhere, as well as to organizations in the industrial and commercial fields. Roy is married with three adult children – two sons and a daughter.

# PARADIGM SHIFT

## A scientist's journey
## through experiment to faith

**PROFESSOR ROY PEACOCK**

**Authentic**

19  18  17  16  15  14  13    7  6  5  4  3  2  1

First published 2013 by Authentic Media Limited
52 Presley Way, Crownhill, Milton Keynes, MK8 0ES.
www.authenticmedia.co.uk

**British Library Cataloguing in Publication Data**
A catalogue record for this book is available from the British Library

ISBN 978-1-78078-098-6
978-1-78078-099-3 (e-book)

Cover Design by David Smart
Printed and bound by CPI Group (UK) Ltd., Croydon, CR0 4YY

## To Elizabeth

This memoir is not just my story – it is Elizabeth's too. As wife and mother, she has dedicated herself unstintingly to all I have attempted around the globe. Hers was not always the exciting part, since much of her time was at home, praying for what I was up to and what I intended. Seeing her in the vision the Lord gave me of heaven (of which I write here) serves to underline her centrality in all of our experience with the God we serve.

# Contents

# A Note from the Author

Throughout my life I have endeavoured to record observations with integrity, honesty and accuracy – both in the laboratory and in life generally. When it comes to seeing God at work, often as a result of prayer, I have deliberately kept my notes to a minimum, since my goal has never been to set myself up as some kind of expert, or draw attention to 'my ministry', but simply to put on record some of the extraordinary things that God has graciously allowed me to witness.

In view of this, and mindful of the fact that certain secondary details can be forgotten or conflated over the years, I have avoided the temptation to fictionalize my narrative, preferring instead to leave out details I cannot recall and concentrate on the main event each time – a healing, a provision, or an extraodinary revelation. We tend to call these 'miracles'(a term I discuss in the book) and, if these stretch the belief system of the reader, for that I make no apology.

# Preface

I remember when Elizabeth, my wife-to-be, said yes. She was sitting on a park bench overlooking one of England's most spectacular views: the Avon Gorge crossed by Brunel's Clifton Suspension Bridge. She could not have envisaged the path in life that we would tread together. Yet the view from that bench gave a clue, representing a powerful mix of nature's beauty and science's triumph.

By the grace of God my life has followed a course that has demonstrated a similar synthesis. I offer this memoir to help those on both sides of a divide which need not plague us as it does: to those in the scientific community who base their lives on reason and the careful examination of evidence; and to those who order their lives upon faith and spiritual experience. I cannot deny that there is a battle going on between these two world views, but I do believe that resolution is possible.

When you have read about my life, you may feel the same.

# 1.

# A Career in *What?*

No one sets out in life with the intention of becoming a thermodynamicist. Small boys dream of becoming firemen, superman figures, or spacemen. Big boys yearn to become racing car drivers, athletes, or sportsmen. And then with adulthood comes the ambition to move steadily to the top of the ladder at work.

I was no exception, although my route into adulthood was as singular as the next man's. For me, it all began because I had curly hair. When I was about eight my parents had determined that some religion would do me good, and I was duly despatched to church on Sunday. Almost immediately I was spotted as a potential choir-boy, with no merit other than the hair. This led to another choir which paid me by awarding a scholarship to the local Cathedral School at the age of ten. At no time did I learn to read music: emulating the sounds of my fellow choristers proved sufficient.

School yielded a vital interest in art and rugby, and art became my intended career. But it soon became apparent that I was unlikely to become the next Picasso, or even scratch a living with it. So, with my father's prompting, I took on a five-year apprenticeship at a company making aero-engines. My initial aim was to work at a drawing board: using a pencil might yet satisfy the closet artist in me.

Even so, as I worked my way through engineering workshops, I was soon hooked, and nothing could compare with being part of the team controlling one of the engine test cells. It was here I first saw power being generated – raw power emanating from a complex piece of machinery into which fuel was being fed. For me, excitement and terror lived alongside each other, as over time I saw a set of notes, calculations, drawings and blueprints turn into a piece of hardware doing its job with pleasing smells and a high level of noise.

The terror came when I had to come up really close to the beast. Engines were mounted in closed cells where they were isolated and locked before use. Officially members of the team were not allowed back in until everything was shut down. Having first fired it up and run it for a while, we measured the engine's performance at a safe distance. Then the engine was closed down and the cell doors unlocked.

That at least was the procedure according to the carefully worded safety instructions. The reality was far more memorable.

Gas turbine engines are fitted with things called bleed valves which open and close at predetermined operational points. They are controlled by hand-set screws which, on the design of our particular machine, could only be reached by physically lying across the engine. Adjustment was supposed to involve closing the engine down, unlocking and opening the very large reinforced doors, waiting for things to cool down, changing the screw position, then reversing the procedure – a fine way to lose a precious hour of work. The team had a better idea, one which substantially inflated their bonuses! The apprentice, that junior member of the team who never had the liberty to say no, was put into the cell and sat astride the engine, screw-driver in hand, while the cell was isolated and the engine run up. At the appropriate moment signals through a reinforced window encouraged the apprentice to alter the screw position while the engine ran.

I was the apprentice.

There is little more terrifying than feeling 20,000 horse-power rumbling just under the seat of your pants, as the engine rotates at over 9,000 revs a minute.

Part of the schedule for an apprentice was to attend various classes to teach him his science. One was a course in Applied Heat – that was the name given to Thermodynamics for people like me who couldn't spell the word. Even after five years of study, punctuated by annual examinations, Thermodynamics confused me.

My established and carefully honed method of preparing for examinations was, after a year or so of doing very little study, to cram during the final hours, even to the point of reading up on my way to the exam while seated on public transport. And there was one subject I feared above all – Applied Heat. Even so, I followed my usual tactic. As I sat reading on the upper deck of the bus for my final exam, I ran across a couple of examples which seemed to me to be typical exam material. So I learned them by heart.

The set paper was for three hours, five questions to be attempted. I knew that the pass mark was 40% and to get that figure was likely to be a struggle for me.

Students filed into their numbered spaces, the tension in the room was high and total silence reigned. 'Gentlemen,' (no ladies were present), 'you may turn your scripts over now.'

This was always a heart-challenging moment. As I glanced down the eight questions in total so that I could order their priority, it suddenly dawned on me that the two questions from the upper deck of the bus were right there on the paper in front of me. Numbers were different but the wording, the method of attack and the solution, were exactly the same. Twenty minutes later, with two hours and forty minutes remaining, the two questions were completed and I knew that I had passed the examination. With only three questions now remaining to be done in over two-and-a-half hours, I couldn't avoid doing outstandingly well.

So, with as yet no real understanding of the subject but an astonishing examination result, I was declared to be a thermodynamicist. My career was set!

Early days in a range of workshops proved educational, not least through the highly adjectival Anglo-Saxon my co-workers employed to communicate. One man in particular had a language skill that fascinated me – I enjoyed talking to him just to count the number of cusses he could fit into one sentence. (For the record, it was nine.)

But the most serious aspect of training at that time was, for me, distilled into a single day's experience. It was proving to be a regular day on the shop-floor until a rumour went round that the prototype of the company's new aircraft, the Bristol Britannia, had undershot the runway on landing and was stuck in a field. That seemed to me to be a great wheeze and a sight not to be missed. I could picture the aircraft, under-carriage stuck deep in a field of Brussels sprouts, the pilot and crew standing around with hands in pockets, looking embarrassed, not sure how to explain what must have been a simple error by the pilot. I had to see this.

A bicycle was borrowed and, guessing the flight path of the aircraft on its final approach, I cycled furiously in that direction. To my surprise it was several miles before I arrived at the scene. I looked around. Small groups of people, silenced by the trauma of what they had witnessed, were standing around and saying nothing: there was nothing they could say. There was no aircraft, no crew, nothing that I could recognize other than a mangled engine leaning against the wall of a house in a row of houses. There was a dent in the ground close to an unexpected gap between two houses, and the whole area was scattered with fairly small pieces of metal.

The day before, a house had stood where the dent was.

The aircraft had disintegrated, leaving nothing more than its thumb-print in the ground and a paper-chase of metal bits and pieces mixed with small bits of masonry. But where was the crew? That was when I saw the body bags, black and heavy, being reverently carried away as men stood by and raised their hats and bowed their heads in silence.

The effect on me was dramatic. Slowly I returned to my borrowed bicycle and wearily pedalled back to the workshops with the noise and the Anglo-Saxon of those who had not seen the tragedy. My mind was trying to grasp what I had just witnessed. Men had gone that morning to a meeting at a runway to experience a demonstration of the new technology – the captain, the co-pilot, the air crew, the company sales team and the team of the purchasing company. But they would never return home, never greet their wives, children and friends . . . all because of what was rumoured eventually to have been a simple assembly fault in the aircraft control system.

This all came down to people – good but fallible people. The error of maybe just one man and one inspector had had a massive result. If so much could depend on one man, then I knew that some day, somewhere, lives could depend on me.

It was then that I made a promise to myself: science in general and engineering in particular would no longer be a fun game for scoring points against colleagues, no more a sport in which the winner took the prize. This would be a serious matter for me; I would work in the best way I knew how. Previously I had been a child playing childish games, but now there was a new challenge: to be a man.

The awful sense of that day has never left me. Things had the potential to go catastrophically wrong, and one day it could be my job to see they went right.

This was a turning point in my life.

I had known Elizabeth for many years, from before I had begun to explore a career of any form. Her interests were not in any scientific subject – just as well, or life would have been pretty boring. Our wedding, standing beneath a huge sculpture by Jacob Epstein, *The Majestas*, took place in South Wales, the 'land of my father-in-law' as I have loved to call it ever since, and it was from there that, leaving the comfort of industry, I went to become a post-graduate research student.

Some years later, at Cambridge, we were at the St John's College May Ball, a particularly jolly affair where we exercised our Royal Prerogative to eat swan at dinner. Elizabeth noticed one couple on the dance floor who seemed to her quite different. She discovered that he was the Chaplain of St John's College (and was later to become the Bishop of Lichfield). In the midst of this noisy, rather raucous, alcohol-enriched evening, she was struck by a sense of purity shared by both of them. Spiritually, my own life had been moving away from anything religious towards a form of atheism, while Elizabeth maintained a wistful memory of her childhood with its church activity. But now, seeing this couple behaving so differently from those around them, she longed to have what they had.

A few weeks into our married lives Elizabeth and I were invited to a wedding in Sheffield. This was a joyous family occasion for all who were there – except for me, that is. For by now my research work lay in shreds on the floor. In fact to me, as I eyed my future as a scientist from the depths of a deep depression, everything seemed to be lost.

Yet this was to be another turning point in my life.

My interests in engineering had been moving towards the narrower field of how fluids behaved within thermodynamic processes – always with an application in mind. The first step was to undertake my first research project, in which I evaluated the performance of a type of engine known as a ducted rocket. This was nothing more than a liquid fuelled rocket engine wrapped up within a ramjet engine, both burning their own fuel, adding their own contribution – and noise – to the overall performance. Now, the importance for application was this: an engine could now potentially operate *both* within the earth's atmosphere where there is oxygen for use *and* beyond the atmosphere. (At this point in the 1950s, inter-planetary travel remained a dream yet to be realized.) Getting to grips with this involved my next step, which was to take me to Cambridge.

To pursue the ducted rocket research I was awarded not one but two supervisors. One was a man of substantial intellect, a deep-thinking, chain-smoking, academic colossus with a very large forehead containing what was evidently an unusually large and active brain. He inspired awe and fear in all those who knew him. The other supervisor was a short, easy-going individual for whom supervisions might well be in the college bar where he would talk about little else than soft landings on Mars and the temperature of the ale being served. Talking about the former was a particularly challenging feat unless, as we were to discover, the bar kept everyone well fuelled and Mars was kept somewhat out of focus.

My big problem was to create a mathematical model of the mixing exhaust flows of a rocket and a ramjet. Over his beer my Mars-landing supervisor offered his priceless advice: 'Just lump the two combustion processes together and the maths will sort itself out.' Brilliant! It was the stuff of inspired leadership, when a sharp, analytical mind that had been scientifically honed got to the root of the matter with precision and simplicity. Or not.

Soon afterwards I was scheduled for a meeting with the other supervisor – the one we all approached on bended knee. 'How is it going?' he asked mildly. I began my presentation enthusiastically enough, only to be interrupted by the question, 'So what have you done about the two zones of combustion . . . the chemical differences and the flow mixing?' No problem – I had my answer ready, just as it had been given me by my other supervisor. Suddenly, the man before me was galvanized. His whole demeanour changed. Leaping to his feet, he waved his hands in the air, pointed accusingly at me and then – leaving behind his carefully controlled academic aura – shouted, 'You fool! You absolute fool! What on earth have you been doing? What have you been thinking?'

Seeing my confusion, he spat out, 'Entropy, man, entropy! You've not accounted for the entropy in the cycle. The two zones operate at different entropy levels – that appears nowhere in your thinking. This is rubbish, total rubbish!'

I left his office in a state of total confusion. My defence that I was only following the direction of the other supervisor was no defence at all, of course. Entropy and a trivial understanding of it had been my downfall. I withdrew from the field of play, battered and without any knowledge of what I should do. A return to his office would be like leaving the trenches again, only this time without a gun and in the full knowledge that the enemy had machine guns trained on my fox-hole! And a return to the other supervisor was out of the question – he might as well have been *on* the planet Mars, such was his accessibility.

It was a pretty dismal weekend for me, despite the happy family wedding. After lengthy discussions with Elizabeth the choice was very simple: either I could do the obvious thing, pack up my Master's Degree thesis, leave the Institute and get back into industry, returning to a fairly mundane life; or I could spend the remaining three weeks before the submission date re-writing the theory from scratch, doing the computer programming and running the results. Quite impossible, but at least I would go down with guns blazing.

Over the next three weeks things were pretty desperate. Every student was allocated one secretary to do the typing and bind the thesis ready for submission. I used two secretaries, full time. I allowed myself no time off, restricted myself to one hour's sleep a night, and only stopped briefly for meals.

It was, as the Duke of Wellington said after the Battle of Waterloo, 'a close-run thing'. The final typing was completed and the last pages bound in with just fourteen minutes to spare. I handed in the finished copies and got them signed for, and then wandered off in a daze to meet fellow student John. He was just off to the bar to celebrate.

As I lay on his bed, waiting for him, I fell into a deep sleep. When he got no response from me, John laid a wet flannel on my face and went in search of company at the bar. Chatting with other students he was asked the question, 'Where's Peacock, then?'

'Oh, I've left him sleeping soundly on my bed. Nothing will wake him up. I put a wet flannel over his face before I came to the bar.'

'You did what?' shouted someone. 'You've probably killed him!'

Having been informed that a sleeping person can't breathe through a wet cloth, John ran the considerable distance back to his room, burst in, saw me lying there exactly as he had left me and, not surprisingly, panicked. Thus I awoke to a voice shouting, 'Roy, Roy, wake up!' while being shaken violently. I lived!

While I am not the first victim in history of a misunderstanding of the effects and application of entropy, I will not be the last. Students of science through the generations are condemned to its malignant effects. But there are far greater consequences stemming from its influence, as our tale shall reveal in due time.

But for now, as I reviewed what happened over that period, I was left with a number of questions. In particular I was puzzled how, having spent a year making such a comprehensive mess of my understanding of the basics of science, I could have started again and, from a clean sheet of paper, completed the project from scratch in three weeks.

And that was not all. When the examination results were announced, notices were posted in public on an Institute Notice Board where the grade of every student was listed, the list being headed by the top mark and so progressively downward. I recall reading the list from the bottom upwards, convinced that, at best, I might creep in with a bare Pass. I rapidly became despondent when I could not find my name anywhere. I reached the top of the list, and there it was! I was speechless. I read and re-read the list, oblivious to the general racket, the cheering and the laughing around me. But there was no doubt: every time that I got to the top of the list, it said, 'Peacock Roy – First Class'. I was stunned. I had been awarded the top mark of the year in my department.

Never in my life had I known anything like this. My name had always propped up the list; the only other time it was at the top was the moment when I had done the Applied Heat exam. What on earth was going on? I began to wonder whether, in the words of an eighteenth-century philosopher, 'there was a hidden hand at the windlass'. Was there perhaps more to life than my science had yet revealed, a dimension that could not be accommodated by the scientific rationalism I was learning?

Searching out the answer to that question set me on an adventure that continues to this day.

# 2.

# On the Outside Looking In

Cambridge is different. It looks different, with its outstanding and eclectic architecture, its colleges arranged in open squares known as courts enclosing immaculate lawns. And it has its own peculiar rules and customs, as I was soon to discover.

Entry to the college building was via a small passage in which the Porter's Lodge stood sentinel. Every college and every court proclaimed its unique nature and history: this was where Isaac Newton laid down the principles of Newtonian mechanics, and over there, next door, William Wilberforce agonized over the reality of slavery. And, gazing imperiously across Trinity Street at the scene beneath him, Henry VIII stood foursquare, as he had down through the centuries, carrying the symbols of his royal commission: in one hand an orb and in the other . . . a chair leg! Every generation of students, it seemed, produced folk who were impossibly serious while others were insufferably jolly. This fact was confirmed to Elizabeth and me immediately after arriving at this shrine to full-on learning and enjoying life.

University rules of residence had developed over the centuries so that, progressively, as students filled the capacity of

the college rooms, arrangements were made for undergrad-
uates to live in lodgings within a radius of three miles of the
front door of Great St Mary's Church on the town square.
By the time I got to Cambridge, this limit was extended to
ten miles for graduates. It goes without saying that, ignorant
of the quaint rules that go to make up Cantabrian life, I had
purchased a house that was 10.3 miles from Great St Mary's.
This was a matter of crisis for my legally minded tutor, who
had to arrange a special dispensation from the university to
permit me to live outside the limit.

My college tutor, a lawyer, was quite irritatingly pedantic
over the minutiae of the university and college laws. And yet
the heat created by the problem of the rogue 528 yards that
separated me from the lawful was nothing compared with
the apoplexy generated in the good man when it was found
that I had gone away for the weekend without signing an
*exeat*. Disapproval became a regular feature of college life,
with the result that I was required to produce a weekly signa-
ture from my 'lodging-house keeper' declaring that I was in
my lodgings and my room by 10.00 p.m. daily. In order to
line up with college regulations, my wife was declared to be
my lodging-house keeper!

It was at the beginning of this saga that Elizabeth and I
were invited to dine with my tutor in his rooms, an event
carefully arranged by our host who also invited another
married couple for the occasion. As both couples had their
first newborn child, a lively conversation was guaranteed.

We met standing over the tray of sherry in the candle-lit
dining room of the tutor's set of rooms. The other student
opened the play by introducing himself: 'Smith-Carruthers –

Eton and the Life Guards.' As he spoke he stood to attention and bowed slightly – stiffly from the hip and with a discernible click of the heels. I could see he was a pro at this sort of activity from the fact that he accomplished the manoeuvre without so much as a stir in the meniscus of his sherry. I wasn't sure how to respond, though I did manage to spill some of my own. In the event I didn't need to dazzle anyone with my powers of conversation, since the Smith-Carruthers were more anxious to talk about themselves and their family than to waste time on anything else, least of all us. Soon they were mapping out their son's future.

'We are probably sending him to the Dragon in Oxford – a good feeder for Eton later on. From there we shall be sending him here to Cambridge – to St John's where he will read law. He will enter Chambers in London as a barrister. Our plan is that he take silk and become a judge as a preliminary to his career in the High Court.'

Smith-Carruthers Junior was all of three months old. I was dumbfounded! What was our ambition for our son? Put simply, it was to hope he would soon learn not to fill his nappy, and also get on to solid foods quickly – far cheaper for his impoverished parents. In the circumstances I determined to keep my mouth shut, to escape as soon as possible and look elsewhere for social contacts.

Social contacts were found, in particular at the Societies Week, a time when all of the university clubs and societies displayed their wares to attract the new student entry into membership. I was wooed by the College Rugby Club, the Cricket Club, the Chess Society, the Hockey Club and every sort of sport conceivable. Among the less physically demanding organizations was the Christian Society, a small group of sincere and, in my view, totally deluded men and women who offered the unsuspecting passer-by orange juice, biscuits, cakes and plenty of conversation with a prospect of heaven. Who was I? What was my college affiliation? Did I live in college? Had I ever thought seriously about Christianity and its claims? Had I ever read the Bible? What was my view regarding Jesus Christ? Had I considered the possibility that I might have a relationship with him? Would I like to know Jesus?

Although penetrating, the questions and the implicit challenges were put so gently that it was impossible to get into a combative mood. There was no foothold for my pet arguments, no chance to assert myself, no discernible path to making a killer statement; everybody was far too nice for that. The only strategy for me at this point was to remember a pressing engagement and absent myself.

Yet, of all the visits and conversations I had that day, this was the one that stayed with me.

Research students normally had desks in communal offices that housed up to six occupants. In my case, I shared with an anglicized Pole who was intent on a career in academia to pursue work in fluid mechanics (he was last heard of running a company that made escalators and lifts), another Pole (who did not speak English) from the Warsaw Institute of Technical Problems doing work in reinforced concrete, a South African who would not talk about his work, an Englishman doing fancy things with boundary layers and who was also very interested in old motor cars (a subject that drew us together), a British Army officer whose research in electro-osmosis involved freezing ground over large areas . . . and me, now working in the field of three-dimensional viscous flows in curved channels. Our discussions always covered a wide range of subjects, usually migrating to the matter of solving the maths surrounding our individual problems.

That is, with the exception of the Army officer, an irrepressibly jolly man who made a lot of noise with his very big boots as he marched up and down the corridor and around the office. After a few weeks it became evident that his agenda was different.

He invited Elizabeth and me to tea with him and his wife. She turned out to be as happy an individual as her husband, with an outgoing nature that encouraged conversation.

So what were we going to talk about? Electro-osmosis? Fluid mechanics? Not very thoughtful with the ladies present. His college and my college, then – life in the department we shared? But no. To my total astonishment the subject to which they kept returning – as faithfully as the needle on a compass swinging back to North – was their church. It was the only subject which absorbed, excited and filled their minds. Last Sunday had seen a very inspiring set of anthems, next Sunday involved the local scout troop marching into the service to present their colours at the altar. It seemed that every week had some highlight that, as they explained it, really should have made the national news.

Elizabeth and I were silenced, cornered with no immediate means of escape. Once we did manage to scurry back to our car, I muttered to Elizabeth, 'They are mad, totally mad.' From then on, whenever those big boots came pounding down the corridor towards my office, I could be seen rushing off to a meeting that needed my input and simply would not wait for me. From that moment, contact with our erstwhile hosts never got beyond a rushed hello over my shoulder as I disappeared through the door and over the horizon.

So here I was, part of one of the greatest seats of learning in the world, where conversation should be guaranteed to be of a clinical, objective and definitive nature, where life could be described in a series of mathematical statements and everything was reducible to a set of universally agreed axioms, yet finding myself repeatedly running into people with odd, non-definitive ideas described in subjective terms that were always just beyond my grasp.

Matters came to a head, not in the rarefied atmosphere of the university department, but in the village in which we lived – 10.3 miles beyond the style of argument that university life demanded. My daily journey to and from Cambridge was necessarily by car. In my case, this meant several cars consecutively but never more than one at a time, some of which didn't work for most of the time and others for none of the time. Every car had cost no more than sixty pounds, and to make it work demanded a quality of mechanical engineering hard learned in my apprenticeship.

On the occasion that became the fulcrum of my story, I was lying under the car of the moment, trying to sort out the clutch levers, when I heard a heavy foot-fall on the path. From beneath the car, I could see a large pair of heavy shoes, the trousers an inch short of the shoe: a farmer, I presumed. I emerged from beneath the car to meet a big, tall man who introduced himself as David. David wanted me to know about the mission coming to the local church in a week or so's time. I wanted to get on with my job.

'Church? Oh, that's my wife's department. Ring the front door bell and she will answer.' As he complied I disappeared beneath the car once more.

After nearly an hour it occurred to me that I hadn't noticed the man leave. Going to the house, I saw that David was standing in the hallway talking earnestly with Elizabeth. The upshot of this was that we were committed to going to the mission.

But not before another member of the village had had a go at me.

George Griffiths was a retired clergyman whom I liked hugely, being an entertaining conversationalist. We talked about many subjects, especially antique furniture and old pewter (an abiding passion of his), but we always avoided anything that would lead us to religion. Still, I knew that this man was dangerous and clearly a little mad – although he was retired he still wore a black jacket and, worst of all, a dog collar. I had concluded that anyone who wore a dog collar one minute beyond the contracted time had to be potty and that one day, inspired by his deep-seated madness, he would try to get me.

That day arrived. 'Why is it that you never come to church, Roy?' I had my answer, carefully rehearsed.

'George, I'd love to come to church, but you see, it's quite impossible. We have two very small children, we live 160 miles from our nearest relatives, we don't know folk locally. So we can't arrange baby-sitters.' That had surely dealt with the matter and excused us for ever from such a tiresome challenge.

'That's wonderful,' George responded. 'We have a crèche every Sunday morning, so you can bring your children along, leave them in the crèche, then come to the service and enjoy yourself for an hour.'

Church service? Enjoy yourself? I had never heard these words used in the same sentence before. Worst of all, there was no escape from the beguiling invitation. Normally I was at home in the cut and thrust of academic debate, the point-scoring, the destruction of an adversary's arguments, the triumph of leaving the other side speechless; but now I was in unfamiliar territory: I was not in control.

So it was decided. We went to church, which proved a rather jolly occasion to everyone except me. I found it a weird experience.

We went through the preliminaries, sorting out a variety of books, brochures and pamphlets. We all read or sang from these documents as directed. We were led in prayers in which I was required to confess that I was a miserable sinner. (If I hadn't felt a miserable sinner before, I was certainly being propelled towards that mindset now.) But all was not lost – within moments I learned that I was, in any case, forgiven, so I could be happy. I was guided rapidly through a series of emotions in which I was sad, I was happy, I was a sinner, I was free, I was under conviction, I was not . . . a roller coaster in which I sat, I stood, I knelt, my head was down, my head was up, my eyes were closed and then were open.

We arrived at the sermon, clearly the centrepiece of events. The minister climbed the steps to the pulpit, led the congregation in a short prayer, and then invited his hearers to be seated. There was a noticeable sense of anticipation when he began speaking. He began with a joke. I was thunderstruck! Then he compounded his felony by laughing at his own joke. Finally, he got so excited that he began waving his hands around as if he were flying.

There I was, serious in my atheism, ready to be convinced but even more ready to argue my corner and demonstrate conclusively the improbability, nay, the impossibility of God's existence, and all that was presented to me were the meanderings of a deranged comedian.

We drove to Bury St Edmunds for lunch, where I maximized my opportunities to describe events in our village. Upon our return home that evening I was to discover a hand-delivered letter on our doormat. Would we like to come for supper on the next evening? I was a student and we lived a marginal existence, so the thought of a good meal was very attractive. Looking at the end of the letter it was immediately established that our hosts were okay – good food was assured. But then I read the last part. If we could join them for supper, we should meet our hosts beforehand at the mission service. The unspoken comment was clear: no mission, no supper. For a student to whom good meat on a plate was a rare blessing, the offer was not to be refused. We went to the mission meeting.

The main event of the evening took the form of a film. *Souls in Conflict* was produced by Billy Graham, of whom I had never heard, and consisted of the stories of half a dozen people, all of whom seemed to live pretty miserable lives . . . that is, until they heard Billy Graham preaching when, at a critical point, they got silly grins on their faces and all was well.

There was, however, one man who commanded my attention. He was an engineer. He carried a slide rule in his hand, which dated him and the film but earned my respect, since a slide rule was like an extension of my own right hand. And then this man, who appeared to be my only ally in this sea of nonsense, also fell. As soon as the going got tough he changed sides, silly grin and all.

We left the film and headed off to the supper which we had surely earned. Elizabeth and I were alone in the car. She turned to me and said, 'What did you think of the film, Roy?'

'It was lousy,' was my terse response.

'Now, Roy, Denny and Ian believe that sort of stuff, so if they ask you, you won't be rude to them, will you?'

'If I think that it was lousy and I am asked, I shall say it was lousy.'

'Oh Roy . . .'

We arrived in silence at our promised supper and went in to meet the other participants. I was impressed, mainly by the fact that the sandwiches had the crusts cut off and the coffee was in such small cups I didn't know what to do with my suddenly superfluous fingers. The pleasant conversation about nothing in particular came to a sudden halt when our hostess turned and asked, 'What did you think of the film?' She was addressing me. As every eye turned on me I recalled my promise to Elizabeth and duly replied, 'I thought it was lousy.'

The evening drew to a close rather quickly and we went home. However, the week of meetings continued, till on the Saturday evening Elizabeth was scheduled to be part of the tea-making squad at a social evening. I followed later, to collect Elizabeth and bring her home, but events led to us being cornered by David, the big man with the big boots. He finished up at our home drinking cocoa, and before long the subject of meeting God was raised again. With an air of finality Elizabeth intoned, 'But I shall never be good enough to meet God!'

'You could meet God now. Would you like to pray?' She would and she did. I watched in horror at what might happen.

With the challenge becoming ever clearer, as she bowed her head in prayer, I decided to use my tried and tested scientific investigative methodology to determine whether God existed or not. I could not take a scientific instrument to prove, measure or ascertain God in any way, but I could use inductive methods – just as an astronomer might establish the existence of a black hole indirectly through its gravitational effects.

My wife had asked that God would give her a new life. If he existed and if he was God, then he would be aware of my wife's integrity – to which, I concluded, he would respond: he would give her the new life she was seeking. If there were to be anything different between the new life and what my wife already had, then it must be discernible, otherwise what was its value? Further, the new life being spoken of had to have something attractive and compelling about it, to the point that, if I saw it, I should want it also.

So I watched. In the best scientific way that I could muster I was about to prove, to my own satisfaction, the major question of mankind in history: is God there, can he be known, and what is the consequence? If there is no God, I reasoned, then this prayer for a new life will be to no avail. Elizabeth will be unchanged. On the other hand, if there is a God, and he has heard her prayer, then there will be a fundamental and observable change in her life. That may leave me with a problem whose order was beyond my ability to assess, but so be it.

Elizabeth said goodbye to her past (theologically minded people would say that she repented) and asked for the new life.

Watching this from a distance of a few feet, the scientist in me determined to examine what I was seeing with the detached mind I had been trained to use. Elizabeth and I had known each other over a number of years. We had become so close that I reckoned I knew her mind in all the situations we encountered. Further, I knew that her life was fashioned by truth and integrity. With her head bowed in prayer I watched in astonishment as this woman – my wife – spoke to God. I listened to her side of the conversation, as she explained that she now understood she was a sinner and was asking God to forgive her. Then she asked God to take away her old life and give her a new one.

Before me was the perfect experiment. I knew well the initiating conditions, the character and nature of the woman to whom I had been married for some years and whom I had known for many more. Next I needed a perturbing force of some sort, so that I could subsequently draw a conclusion in comparing measurements, before and after.

So I watched carefully. Elizabeth had asked for a new life – that request was the perturbing force in my experiment. Now I needed to examine the result.

Would she look up as she had looked down? If so, I would readily conclude that the result of the perturbing force, her cry to God, was zero: God did not exist.

On the other hand, if she was manifestly different when she looked up, I would begin to wonder whether her prayer had been answered and whether there might be a God who had answered it.

She looked up and already I had my answer. Her countenance was radiant. Something of fundamental importance had happened to her and she was changed.

And that meant I had a problem.

# 3.

# Paradigm Shift

My calculating scientific methodology had led me to a point where I had not wished to arrive. It appeared God might exist after all; and that he could impact people's lives and bring about an identifiable change in them. And from where I was standing, that change was looking good!

But evidence for God's existence can bring more than one reaction in a person's life. Certainly a glance had made this observer hungry for all that an encounter with God might involve. Yet I could see already that such an encounter would cost something.

Old things must pass away so that all things might become new. The old things – old habits, old way of life, even old friendships – come under scrutiny in the light of the claims God makes upon our lives. And some of these old ways are valuable to us.

So here was my challenge: in simple terms, was I prepared to give up all things, little knowing that I would become the heir of all things? Recalling my church-going youth, and that recent mission event, I was aware that it was necessary to confess I was a miserable sinner. But, truth to tell, I was not even remotely miserable! I actually enjoyed the life I led, sinner or not. No one seemed to understand that, while in their language I was a sinner, I was a happy one. I chose a lifestyle which brought me pleasure – nothing miserable about that and, until I met the One who didn't sin, until I discovered His life and chose to follow Him, I didn't even know what sin was.

So: call it what you wish . . . life of sin or life of pleasure . . . could I give up that life? That was a big call.

Yet the challenge of Elizabeth's commitment, as I observed it then and there, made me realize I was in the middle of a set of circumstances over which I had no control. Was there nothing I could do? To change the dynamics of the situation about me I turned from David and addressed Elizabeth. 'Could you make some coffee for us, please?'

This was aimed at defusing the situation by introducing a diversion. But I had committed a huge tactical error. As Elizabeth dutifully went to the kitchen, I was left alone with the madman who had been controlling the conversation and pursuing an agenda of which I knew nothing. And David now turned his attention to me.

'You're not going to get me on your emotional high tide,' I said with as much authority as I could muster.

'I can see that,' he responded and, although he tried, he couldn't gain any traction in his argument before Elizabeth returned with a tray of coffee. It was not long before I was manoeuvring him through the front door.

Maybe that was an end to the matter after all. Life might now return to normal and I could get on with pursuing, uninterrupted, my research into secondary distributed vorticity in viscous flows, all in the peaceable world where I

sat at my desk playing with the mathematics of the phenomenon under inspection, drinking coffee and eating cream
buns in the Common Room in the Department at the heart
of Cambridge.

But it was not to be. I did not allow for the radiant look
on Elizabeth's face, the 'silly grin' as I had previously referred
to it. To my dismay, it didn't go. When we went to bed Elizabeth was still sporting her grin. It seemed to me she wore it
as a trophy.

For me, bed has always been a matter of switching off.
Sleep comes easily. But on this night it was not to be. My
situation was made the more irritating in that I could hear
Elizabeth's regular breathing beside me. It is in a moment
like this that one is tempted to reach out with a foot, prod
one's neighbour, and wake her up to apologize profusely for
disturbing her: 'Did I wake you? Oh dear . . .' But around
three o'clock that morning, with still no sign of sleep to
disrupt the storm inside my head, something happened that
blew away any such wicked intentions. Not knowing the
correct terminology to describe things I could only say that,
in the blackness of the bedroom, with no lights from inside
or out, no moon or street illumination, I saw a picture. I
would now call it a vision.

The scene before me was of a very large field, viewed over
a four-feet-high trimmed yew hedge, and stretching as far as
a near horizon that was defined by a row of elm trees. It was
autumn time and the leaves of the trees were almost black,
just before they turned brown with the season. The field itself
had been sown with wheat, but had been harvested leaving
stubble across the area. The stubble lay in uniform rows

of about five feet, as the harvester had left it, well defined strips of light and dark brown stretching to the horizon. The nascent artist in me responded to this well-groomed sight. Then, to my left and at a distance of about twenty-five feet on the further edge of the field, I saw, waving in the wind, a single strand of wheat that the combine-harvester had missed.

I looked at this strand of wheat with some sorrow. The farmer had planted the seed; the seed had germinated; the shoot had grown, eventually to full height; new grain had appeared at the top of the plant; the grain had grown to full size; it had swollen out and ripened; it was ready for the harvest. But it was too late. The harvester had passed and missed it. The wind would come and it would blow over. The rain would follow and the stalk with its grain would rot. It was as good as dead already.

It was then that the full horror of what I was seeing struck me. As if by a revelation, I knew that the stalk of wheat was me. Had I been prepared for a harvest in the week of the mission? But now the mission was effectively over. Maybe it was too late.

And then I heard a voice, audibly and not in my head, as if someone were speaking to me. The voice said, quite firmly, 'The harvest is past, the summer is ended, and we are not saved.' I wasn't given to hearing voices in the night, so who could this be? Then, speaking louder, the voice repeated, 'The harvest is past, the summer is ended, and we are not saved.' By now I was fully alert, listening intently for any movement, anything to disclose the presence of someone around me.

Then again: 'The harvest is past, the summer is ended, and we are not saved.'

There could be no doubt about it. This God, in whom I did not believe, about whose existence I was prepared to have arguments with my philosophically inclined friends, and who did not communicate with his creation, was actually speaking to me. But what was he saying? What has passed? What has ended? What is it to be saved? It was many months later that I learned that those words were already to be found in the Bible (see Jeremiah 8:20).

I was now terrified. I was terrified at the prospect of God's existence, and terrified that he was speaking to me, and terrified of what he was saying. 'The summer is ended.' If there was any sense in what I was experiencing, it had to mean that an opportunity was being missed, and the consequence was that I was not saved.

My wife had received the God who had offered himself. I had rejected all that I had heard, even in church when I had read the right words and been a member of the right organizations. My wife was in but I was out. Could I do anything about it? Certainly, in that darkness before the dawn, I wanted to.

Morning came after only a couple of hours' sleep. In that cold autumn daylight things seemed a little different. I needed to pull myself together, get back into that familiar territory of analytical thinking that would despatch the strange excursions of my mind.

It was Sunday and Elizabeth announced that she was going to church. This was my moment to assert myself and be my own master. 'I'm changing the gearbox in the car,' I replied. So off she went to church, while under the vintage Riley I crawled, dragging my toolkit to loosen the gearbox from its fixings. An hour and a half later Elizabeth returned, her face alight at what she had experienced. 'Roy, you must go this evening,' she declared.

What else could I do?

The building was only half full, making it a little more difficult to hide behind the person in front. The hymns were not memorable and the missionary was someone to whom I had taken quite a personal distaste. This was not the perfectly set stage for a spiritual encounter of any kind, but I hid as well as I could, not behind a pillar since that would have been rather an obvious ploy, but at least half out of view of the speaker. (I have seen this technique used by others many times since, when I have been speaking, and take it that these are precisely the people at whom to aim my prayers and my challenges.)

I may have slid down in the pew to become invisible, but it was with discomfort and then horror that I recognized every statement made by the missionary to be directed at me personally – even though this was not clear to the congregation. It was my life being laid out; these were my problems being explained; it was the emptiness in my life that was being highlighted. And it was the offer of a relationship with Jesus Christ that was aimed at me. For me at that moment everyone else was a bystander.

I had no choice, I must do something about this. The speaker concluded by saying, as he had done all week, 'If anyone wants to know more about Jesus Christ, will they ask me for the little red book as they pass me at the door?'

This time the voice I heard was speaking within me. It was different.

'You don't want to have anything to do with this.'

A second voice replied, again within me. 'But they've got what you want.'

'You are not like them.'

'But they've got what you want.'

'Listen, you are an intellectual. They are all country bumpkins.'

'But they've got what you want.'

'What would your friends at the university think if they knew about this?'

'But they've got what you need.'

It was the change in that one word that did it. Whether I wanted what was on offer was of no consequence; it was what I needed that mattered.

So I did as I was told. I determined to ask for the little red book, but it would be done my way. I wouldn't be seen by the congregation as a penitent sinner. So how could I get my hands on this tiny morsel of writing without acknowledging publically that I actually needed to be saved?

My plan was carefully laid. The missionary was standing to the right side of the door, the remaining members of the congregation were somewhere behind me to my right. I would approach him when there was no one around and say, 'Can I have the little red book please?' I would take the book in my right hand and, just in case he wanted to shake hands, the book would be transferred immediately to the left pocket of my jacket. To transfer the book to the left pocket in my jacket, the pocket flap was pushed in beforehand, and I would turn towards the door obscuring the sight of anyone behind me. Then I would be out of the building. No one would know. My secret would be kept for life and I could pursue whatever relationship God had for me without any observers taking notes.

I awaited my moment, pushed the pocket flap in, cleared my throat and made my way meaningfully and full of authority towards this man. He watched me without blinking, which was a little unnerving. I stood before him – and forgot my lines!

Desperate to break the silence, I said, 'Good evening.' He responded in like manner so I added, 'I'm very interested in what you've been talking about.'

'Oh yes?' he said.

'But then,' I added, 'I have always been a Christian.'

'Oh yes.'

Rats, I thought, if I say I've always been a Christian, how can I now ask him for a book on how to become a Christian?

'Nevertheless, I am interested in the philosophy you employ.'

'Oh, yes.' It seemed he was a man of few words.

'So, can I ask you . . .'

'Yes?' he urged me.

'Can I ask you for the little red book?' A beam of joy broke out on his face as he said with triumph (or so it sounded to me), 'Oh, yes!' As he pulled it from behind his back I looked at the little red book in horror. Red it certainly was, but little? I calculated that it was about eleven inches by fifteen, and my only thought was, I'll never get this into my pocket. But I had to take it.

In that instant my life was changed. Suddenly I had a peace I had never known before, a peace that exceeded my understanding. And I had joy, joy that was inexplicable. And I knew I had a mission in life, even if right then I had no idea what that might be. This I did know, however. I had met God and it was as if I had been washed clean and bathed in his reality. Furthermore, all thoughts disappeared about this being kept to myself, a secret religion where I would live one spiritual life to the exclusion of all others I met. I wanted everyone to know that I had met God. I had undergone the ultimate paradigm shift.

I walked from the church building into a dark night. There was nobody about with whom I could share this revelation.

But I was bursting to tell anyone I met. It was one thing to demonstrate the two laws of thermodynamics, to explore the kinetic theory of gases, to see thermal energy being translated into mechanical work; but this was on a different level. The God of Galileo, of Kepler, of Copernicus, of Clerk-Maxwell and many others . . . He was now my God.

I hadn't done any of the approved things. I hadn't read the right books, hadn't prayed the sinner's prayer, hadn't taken the right hand of fellowship, hadn't signed up to anything. All that mattered was that God had seen my heart and, at the location where the work is really done, he had stood there and welcomed me home.

What had happened to me? It was as if the tectonic plates upon which my life was founded had taken a massive shift. I recall seeing archive photographs taken in Western California along the San Andreas Fault following the 1906 Californian earthquake. Buildings and features of San Francisco as it had previously been were clearly recognizable so, to the San Franciscan, there was no doubt about what was being observed. And yet, familiar as it was, it was manifestly different from what had gone before. The view had been irredeemably altered. And it would have been quite impossible to reverse things, even if you wanted to. I have stood at the Fault in Hollister, California. There it is easily identified by an almost vertical step of over twenty feet, which gives some impression of the energy expended in the event. This is replicated in one street in San Francisco where the fault-line runs down the central reservation in the road, such that cars going north do so at a different height from those going south. Yet the road had been designed and built as a unit, north and south traffic moving at the same level.

The 1906 earthquake had resulted in a reshaping of part of Western California. And now this moment of commitment in my life, standing on some medieval flagstones inside the door of St James Hemingford Grey in the Cambridgeshire fens, had resulted in a spiritual earthquake. I knew that nothing would be the same again.

I had no idea what being 'born again' meant, or 'converted', 'saved', or 'redeemed'. These were theological terms that were meaningless to me. All I knew was that foundations had been shifted.

It was not for some years that I began to discover the relevance of thermodynamics – its application and importance: that all the processes we see in the universe, from the telescope to the microscope, are subject to the constraints of its two laws. It is a fact that the entropy level of the universe will never be the same again as it is in the moment you read this. Entropy continues to increase in spite of anything I may do, and this is an irreversible process; the thermal characteristics of the universe can never return to an earlier configuration. We are aging and we can't get any younger – we cannot relive an earlier life.

Now the thing is: just as physical life is a one-way process, so too is spiritual life. And so this fundamental scientific fact brought me great comfort. Just as I could not reverse entropy, which is a time-related quality, so I could not reverse what had now happened on the stone floor of that church. Conversion – being ushered into the presence of Jesus Christ – was a life-changing experience and there was no way that I could un-change it. I was blissfully unaware that Jesus had said, 'Lo, I am with you always, even to the end of the age.' There was a time when I was blissfully unaware of the implications of entropy, but that didn't alter the demands of the Second Law of Thermodynamics in the slightest. However I looked at it, this conversion I had now experienced had a permanency about it, and this would become one of the foundations in my newly discovered Christian life.

# 4.

# In the Beginning

When someone embarks on the Christian life there is not just a new life to be lived –there is a whole new language to be learned as well. This is not so much about the meanings of certain words, although there is inevitably a degree of theological jargon to circumnavigate. Rather it is in the discovery that the words really mean something – they make a difference to life. Without this element the Christian religion is nothing more than theory. We can learn the language, read the Book and engage in a variety of acceptable activities, but without the experiment of experience we have nothing more than a *hypothesis*.

In this way the lives of the scientist and the Christian have parallels. So, for instance, a theory remains a theory until it has been proved by experiment. Before the experiment we have a proposition, but it is the experimental measurement that conforms to the mathematical model that produces a law. (This is why, incidentally, we refer to Kelvin's 'laws' of thermodynamics and Darwin's 'theory' of evolution.) In my own field, when the results of the theoretical model married up with those harvested from running an engine, at that point I could say conclusively that a theory worked. For a scientist in that moment, life really was worth living.

So it proved to be in the Christian life. I soon discovered that the claims of Jesus Christ can be subject to enquiry using my own life as a sounding board. My experience began to confirm what had been asserted through generations of Christians and by what is recorded in the Bible. And I eventually discerned a parallel to this process in my professional life as well, moving, as I did, between academia and the industrial world.

It is quite normal for an office or study in the academic world to include an extensive bookcase filled with a wide range of books, reports and folios in a large number of patterns and sizes. These are useful for all manner of occasions – not least as an ideal background when a photograph is needed, since this carries the subliminal message, 'I am intelligent, well read and important.' And yes, there was a wall in my office, hung with books in the approved manner. But they were also a good source of ammunition when responding to the more abstruse questions that a student might have.

'How can a turbulent, viscous boundary layer re-laminarize?' might be the question. I would immediately have a couple of references to hand.

'How can I apply the wave equations to a device in which power is being transferred?' The answer, with the supporting mathematics, could be found in the handy tome within reach.

'Read this,' I would say, 'and note the developments carefully. So that you understand the context, begin your reading at Chapter 1, and then the matter will become evident to you.'

In giving this kind of advice to my students I was offering them my guarantee that the volume was correct and entirely reliable. They could depend on the contents: we might say that they could put their lives on it. Bearing that in mind, there was clearly a heavy responsibility on me to ensure the quality, accuracy and reliability of the recommended writing. To do that, you would be entitled to assume that I had read, in detail, every one of these volumes that adorned my office wall.

Frankly, that was not reasonable: I had a large office wall and another full bookcase on the other side of the room! But to validate the authenticity of a book, I did make three checks. I checked the author. If the author had a good reputation, I knew that the document was likely to be without fault. I checked the contents, dipping into various portions of the text as the fancy took me. If what I read lined up with the axioms on which the science was built and gave results that were tenable, then I reckoned that this could be recommended. Finally, I would seek out colleagues who would have read the volume themselves. Among those colleagues there were one or two I knew to be totally reliable, and their recommendation became the final imprimatur I sought.

This turned out to be a remarkably reliable way of checking. If a volume was flawed at any point, one of the checks would show it up, even if the other two appeared to give me a green light.

Now this triangulation of checks turned out to have direct application in the Christian life, but that rather left me with a problem. When I had the privilege of talking to those who had just committed their lives to Christ, I would recommend three courses of action to them:

- cultivate a life of prayer
- get involved in Christian fellowship
- read the Bible regularly, maybe with the support of some Bible-reading scheme.

The encouragement to prayer was simple enough, as was the advice to be involved with other Christians; but reading the Bible was not so simple a matter. From the time that I had first taken a Bible in my hand after surrendering myself to God, I had found a document that intrigued me, excited me and, in a most direct way, spoke to me. My problem, however, came when I read Genesis Chapter 1 – the very first chapter! Frankly, I did not believe it. My scientific understanding, my rationalistic way of thinking, my logic, all spoke against it. As far as I could see, science told a different story, not one involving a week of events, of a man, a woman and the various species appearing from nowhere. I tried all of the arguments that were fielded, but none was remotely satisfactory.

This concern continued for several years, becoming a much greater challenge than even, for instance, the principle of physical healing through prayer.

I was aware of the arguments rejecting outright the story of the Genesis creation, as I was aware of those that supported the Genesis creation story. Frankly, none that I encountered carried an air of certainty and hence authority about them. Could I believe that everything was accomplished in six twenty-four hour periods, and could I argue it with the rationalism I had been trained to use? Could I believe that, in spite of Darwin's work and the claims built around it, the first man and the first woman were created without forebears? But if I did not accept the generally recognized conservative evangelical position, where did that leave me in respect of the Bible? Was I to adopt a tortuous set of propositions and awkward provisos so that I could still acknowledge the primacy of the Bible, yet simultaneously adopt the apparently secure scientific arguments regarding the emergence of *homo sapiens*?

After some years my position eventually began to crystallize on the Bible's place in the scheme of things. This document, I was prepared to state, was the Word of God, so it had a special place in matters. I realized that my argument was not with the story Moses laid down but with the authenticity of the Bible. I had learned – and I had come to recognize – that my revelation of God, of Jesus and of the Holy Spirit would come from the Bible. In fact, any revelation from any other source should at the very least be borne out by the Bible, if not explicitly reflected in it. In short, I found that the Bible was a book about God, giving me the revelation I may expect to have of him and enlightening and confirming anything the Holy Spirit may say. There was no doubt in my mind: this Bible was written with the express purpose of revealing God to me and anyone who reads it.

What was I to do? Amazingly, the confirmation of what the Bible was saying about creation eventually came in a flash. But such a revelation had to wait until after I had become used to Jesus speaking into my life.

I was reading the account of Jesus in dispute over marriage. He said, 'Have ye not read, that he which made them at the beginning made them male and female?' (Matthew 19:4).

His words hit me like a sledgehammer. I read it again and again in amazement. This was Jesus speaking. He wasn't concerned with scoring debating points; he was making simple factual statements. In passing, in the middle of a debate about marriage, he was saying unequivocally that there was a 'beginning' and there was a 'male' and a 'female'.

Now here was my problem. Jesus believed this story regarding creation, and I did not. What was his authority? He was making the statement two thousand years closer to the event than I had been: maybe that gave him a greater authority than me in the matter. But then I reflected further: he had actually been at the event. As the Word of God, the eternal Son of the Father, he had witnessed it all – in fact created it all. I had no qualifications to hold against that! If I could not accept this on the basis that Jesus had said it, I was declaring him to be fallible. In which case, what did he say that I could believe? I would have to conclude that he was mistaken – even possibly a liar.

And so I faced what became the biggest spiritual battle of my life. I realized that my Christian faith stood or fell on this. There was no question of selectively signing up to various tenets of the Christian life, while omitting those with which I had a problem. I could do that no more than I could accept some fundamental scientific axioms and reject those that I found inconvenient or didn't fit the drift of my thinking. No, I must accept all or nothing. Within me a battle was being fought and it would have eternal consequences.

In prayer, I chose.

I could not understand the implications of the step I was taking, but I made my choice, which was to believe what

Jesus said: there had been a Beginning, there had been a man and there had been a woman. I did it by faith, but I did it. The consequences began to take shape over the following days, as my Bible reading took on a new dimension – one that has remained with me ever since.

Over the next few days things began to fall into place. But I still had a problem. If the Bible was written to tell me about God, why were its introductory chapters about the creation of the universe rather than about God? I could not make sense of this; where was the connection with the person of God? Would it not have been rather more sensible to omit the creation story altogether, thus removing one of the historic points of contention within Christianity altogether? As I saw it, what is generally referred to as the Genesis story did not contribute to the developing themes of the Bible.

Following lengthy reflection on the subject I was playing around with some words in my mind. Creation by God . . . God's creation . . . the creation of God. Then it occurred to me that the Genesis story was not primarily about 'the creation of God' but about 'the God of creation'. These chapters were not some kind of scientific primer; they were the first picture we have of God.

The primary aim of Genesis Chapter 1 is to tell us the story of who God is. And so it begins with the outstanding features by which we can know him. This is directly in line with the way we come to know anyone. You, the reader, probably know nothing about me other than what you are deducing from this book, representing my thoughts. You make some enquiries about me and the first thing you 'learn' is that Roy

Peacock has been officially declared to be an area of outstanding natural beauty. Later, as you get to know more, you find that he has warts to make Oliver Cromwell jealous. So a picture builds up of the reality concerning Roy Peacock.

Maybe in the course of events we get to meet, and your thoughts (worst fears!) are confirmed. Now, somewhere in this process you may decide that you 'know' me. Such knowledge has been built upon the foundation of what you first discovered about me and your first impressions when meeting me.

So let's look at the Genesis story, not so much as one of creation but of the Creator, recalling that I see things from the perspective of a scientist and, specifically, a thermodynamicist.

The writer uses Hebrew, and it is unfortunate that the biblical Hebrew loses something in being translated into English. If we take the opening words of this chapter and try to understand the Hebrew record some astonishing things come to light. 'In the beginning,' which appears to be a faithful translation of the Hebrew, implies that there was a beginning and this, of course, finds an agreement with currently held views in the field of cosmology. The Big Bang theory holds to the idea of a point of initiation for the universe some fifteen billion years ago. Bangs, (if this is the best description we can muster in a void through which no noise can transmit) tend to be expansive and there is no doubt that we live in an expanding universe, with everything we see rushing away from everything else.

The distances involved are so huge that we can't detect this movement with our unaided eyes, but we can measure a change in the light these objects emit. We know that as any source of light moves away from the observer it becomes progressively more red (known as 'red shift'), while anything moving towards the observer has a colour shift to the blue end of the spectrum. (This whole phenomenon is known as the Doppler effect.) Now, as we look out into our universe, the almost universal incidence of this so-called 'red shift' tells us that we live in an expanding universe, which is in direct accord with the Big Bang hypothesis.

These data all go to support the biblical report of the creation, not to prove that the Bible is right (it doesn't need that) but to show that science and the Bible are not mortal enemies. As a scientist I do not have to abandon my Christian beliefs or ethics to pursue an atheistic agenda; rather, I can show that there is a synergy between science and the Bible.

There is one further piece of evidence worth examining. In verse 2 of the creation record we read, 'And the earth was without form and void.' Now these are mysterious words and many have wrestled over an understanding of them. The picture becomes much clearer when we find that the Hebrew actually translates as: 'And the earth was an indescribable chaos.'

We all have some idea of what indescribable chaos looks like – some look no further than a child's bedroom! More seriously, I recall the consequences of the IRA bomb in the Baltic Exchange in London; and I remember walking through Bristol after the air raids on the harbour during the Second World War; and, courtesy of TV news, I see what happens in wars today in other parts of the world. It seems that the mess could not get worse than it is, and certainly when everything has been broken, destroyed, or razed to the ground, we are probably right. In scientific parlance we would say that 'entropy has tended to a maximum'. Now, according to the Second Law of Thermodynamics, that is the final terminus to which the universe is irreversibly headed.

The Second Law is irreversible. It is directly connected with the way in which time works, and that doesn't go backwards. It is inevitable that chaos – also quantified as a component within what scientists call 'entropy' – simply increases within a system: so we may say that, within a system in which a process is ongoing, order tends to disorder. If we could conceive a system in which entropy decreases, disorder tending to becoming order, we would have what might be defined as a miracle – though this cannot be admitted within a normal scientific framework. (For a fuller discussion of the Second Law, see the Appendix at the back of this book.)

And yet Genesis says that chaos came at the start, and only later tended towards order. What are we to make of this? Of course, the reader here may discount the Genesis story altogether, complaining it is not reliable. But then we are left in an untenable position. I don't have to believe in God to accept the theory of the Big Bang. There is, after all, quite a body of evidence to support it. I don't need to believe in God to accept the concept of the twenty-four hour day and the relative order of life as we know it. But I cannot escape the fact that it all exists in the way that it does. And yet all of my scientific knowledge says that the Second Law must be fulfilled, unless there is a miracle.

So we are left with the embarrassing fact of an ordered universe whose very existence defies the 'inviolable' Second Law.

God created the universe from scratch – *ex nihilo* – and the evidence is that it was in 'unutterable chaos'. It was into this darkness that God spoke: 'Let there be light.' And from that there resulted a series of events and developments, all resulting from the fact that 'God said'. Every one of these events resulted in the order that arose out of the original primal disorder. In other words, every time that God said 'Let there be . . .' order resulted: there was a reduction in entropy. By definition, then, every time God spoke, a miracle resulted.

From this, we can conclude a primary fact about God – primary not least because it is one of the first things the Bible has to say about him. His handiwork includes the working of miracles. We might try to ignore this if it does not mesh neatly with our fondly-held opinions, or even with the theological tenets of our denomination, but this is unavoidable: the first thing the Bible teaches us about God is that he is a miracle-worker.

In light of what the Genesis story has to tell us as a characteristic of God's person, it amazes me that we go to such lengths, as the representatives of God on earth, to hide what doesn't seem to embarrass him, and we simply ignore this miraculous aspect of the spiritual life that should clearly set the Christian apart from the rest of the world. Of the numerous moral qualities of character that can be demonstrated through the Christian life, every one can more or less be replicated without the need to be a Christian. But miracles present a problem. The miraculous is God's domain – though graciously he chooses to involve people even here in the fulfilment of his purposes.

As we shall see.

# 5.

# On the Move

Moving into the university world and becoming a member of an academic body promised to be very exciting, an experience in which I left behind the back-stabbing practices of industry.

Or not.

I joined a department of twenty-three colleagues where I was initially welcomed, but it wasn't long before I found difficulties with two faculty members. One was academically not strong; the other – a younger man – was looking for a fight. Alarmed at the way things were developing I started to pray for these men. Matters got worse! They learned that I was a Christian, which provided an obvious target for their bile.

Their animosity continued until the day came when there was a rumour around the Common Room that Benny, the younger of my two opponents, had failed to arrive for his lectures. He was eventually found on the Coventry by-pass in his car. He had had a massive heart attack and died at the wheel.

The whole department was affected. Although he didn't seem to be much liked, there was still a bond between members of the Common Room.

But this was not all. Shortly afterwards Clive, my other nemesis, collapsed and was confined to bed. I felt for him and responded immediately to the message that he wanted to see me. I went to his home and found him in bed. He was propped up on a pillow. Every time he began to speak to me, he wept without control. He asked me to hold his hand, which I did. He then told me how he had watched my life in the department. He realized that there was something about my life he wanted and for which right now he was desperate. We prayed together, and he got right with the God he had never met before but who clearly knew all about him. When I left him, he was at peace. He died a couple of days later.

This was my introduction to the world of academic science. I had mixed feelings about it all, but one thing I knew for sure was this: my God was not living in an abstract world; he was where real people were, and that included scientists. And, with thanks in my heart, I could declare that this God was with me. Further, it seemed that, for now at least, this was where the Lord wanted me.

While I was working with Rolls-Royce we lived on the Derby outskirts in an area known as Mickleover. Now that I was moving into the academic arena a house move was necessary. Unwisely I put the sale of our house into the hand of an agent in a different area.

Selling was hard, and the only encouragement we had was short-lived. A couple came to view as soon as our house went on the market. As they said their goodbyes and walked off the drive, Elizabeth turned to me and said quietly, but with confidence, 'They are going to buy the house.'

'How do you know that?'

'Because God has just told me.'

Yet the couple's initial enthusiasm died immediately the husband found that he had a clause in his conditions of employment that said he must live within the boundaries of Derby. Our house was just beyond the city limits.

As the weeks rolled by the house sale became an urgent issue for prayer. We reminded the Lord that we had put the matter in his hands, so we expected him to facilitate matters.

Then God spoke, quite separately, both to Elizabeth and me.

'You claim to have put the house sale in my hands. So why are you keeping it on the books of the agent?'

'Because that's the way that houses sell, Lord.'

'Take the house off the agent's books and I will sell it for you.'

Could we do that? What if we had not actually heard from God and this was all a construct of our fertile minds?

Now it occurred to me that faith is not a guarantee: it is a guide to God's will. My step must be by faith, not ultimately by any form of proof. So, with my heart in my mouth, I did as I felt God had said: I withdrew the house from the agent's books.

We waited.

Nothing changed, so I raised the matter with God once more.

'But I've done as you told me. What should I do now?'

'If you trust me to sell the house for you, why have you left the agent's board on display outside the house?'

'Because if I don't have that there, no one will know that the house is for sale.'

'If you trust me to sell the house for you, then take down the agent's sale notice and I will sell it for you.'

My heart was heavy as I drew the post and sign from the ground – though I was careful to lay the sign down so that anyone on the street outside would see it.

Again we waited. And again, nothing happened.

'Why has the house not sold, Lord?'

'You still do not trust me. Get rid of the sign and then I will sell the house for you.' Wearily, I phoned the ex-agent and had the sign taken away.

'So what do I do now, Lord?'

'Leave the house empty and I will sell it.' I explained that I couldn't do that. Empty houses do not sell easily and, in any case, this was an area where we could not guarantee there would be no vandalism. Beyond that, empty houses were frequently taken over by squatters, and to have that happen would be a disaster.

'Do you trust me?' he asked.

'Yes, Lord. Of course I do.'

Then God said, 'Move out and I will sell the house.' With the greatest hesitation I did so, asking him to give me a word of confirmation. That coincided with a Bible reading in my pattern of study (Ezekiel 12:3): 'Therefore, thou son of man, prepare thee stuff for removing, and remove by day in their sight; and thou shalt remove from thy place to another place in their sight'. That was a tremendous encouragement, so we booked a removal company to take us to our new home down in Bedfordshire.

Our solicitor was not best pleased when he learned what we were doing, but his words were an encouragement. 'As your lawyer I must advise you not to undertake this plan. There is much that can go wrong and you will have no defence in law against anyone. On the other hand, if this is what God has told you to do, then as your brother in Christ I must advise you just to do it, and you will have every support from me.'

Then we waited.

It was several long weeks before something happened. We found a note pushed through our front door from our good friend Pauline, a Christian in Derby who was visiting Bedford. We met up. Before long the conversation turned to the house move.

'Do you remember the neighbour you introduced me to a couple of years ago, back in Derby? Well, I've kept up the contact and do some baby-sitting for her. Early this week they received a telephone call just before they were due to go out, which they passed on to me. The caller was very anxious to know if your house in Derby was still for sale. I said that so far as I knew it was, and they asked me to let you know that they wanted to buy it.'

'Who are these people'? I asked.

'I don't know them at all. All I can say is that they're very anxious to buy the house if it's still for sale. They assure me they'll pay the asking price.'

We met up and immediately agreed the sale. We were curious how they knew so much about the property.

'We've seen it before,' the man said. 'Only when it first came on the market we couldn't proceed because of a contractual clause that forbade me from living outside the city limits.'

Elizabeth was astounded. 'Of course, I recognize you now! You were the first people to view the property.' She took great delight in pointing out to me later on that God had told her right at the start that this couple would buy the house.

But there was another thread to this story, of which we had been unaware. Originally our house had been about a hundred yards outside the city boundary. However, as a result of a petition in Parliament, the MP for Derby South East, George Brown, had successfully had the boundary relocated, and we were now within the city limits. It really impressed me that the Lord was so interested in us making the move that he arranged an Act of Parliament to make it possible!

Selling a house in Derby had its trials, but buying one just north of London proved no easier.

I began house hunting in the usual manner, regularly taking delivery of all the local papers, getting on to the books of every agent in the area and then doing the foot slogging to try to look interested as the vendors, one by one, sought to make a sale with me. Yes, the avocado bathroom suite was delightful, the open staircase was a great fashion statement, the range of wall papers made one delirious with excitement, particularly the Mickey Mouse pattern in one bedroom. Every day's work in the office was brought to a close with the prospect of mandatory viewings of two properties. I hated it.

After two more viewings one evening I was driving disconsolately back to the Cranfield Institute where I had accommodation on site. Driving along a back road in the countryside, I prayed, asking the Lord why he hadn't shown me the house in which we were to live. I recall, with clarity, the left-hand bend in the road I was navigating when he replied, 'I'm not showing you the house because you are not giving me the chance to.'

'Then what should I do, Lord?' Again, he spoke.

'Stop looking for the house and then I will bring it to you.'

This was madness, but I had asked and I had received an answer. I was so far into this pursuit that I decided to do just that. That meant ridding myself of the piles of agents' papers.

Dinner that evening was arranged to be in the refectory where I had promised to meet a friend from another department. I respected Angus highly. We met, found a table and set about the evening meal.

'How's the house-hunting going, Roy? Any positive movements yet?'

'As a matter of fact, I do have something to report.' So saying, I then went over my recent conversation with God. There was a silence, broken at last by the clash of Angus' cutlery being set down on his plate. Then with serious face he said,

'Roy, you know that many of your colleagues are well aware of your spiritual position and are watching what you do. Take a word of advice from me. Just buy a house. It doesn't matter what house or where it is. Buy it, move in and then you can begin the Christian work you are meant to be doing here.'

'Angus, I agree entirely with you, but I am sure that God has spoken to me and I have to obey.'

The domestic halls at the Institute did not have every mod. con. in every room. One thing lacking was a telephone; the only one was on the porter's desk in the entrance hall.

The following week I had an unexpected conversation over coffee with two colleagues in our Common Room. My position as a Christian was the centre of attention.

'But Roy, how do you know that God exists? How can you prove all you claim?' These were serious questions put honestly, not to create conflict. So, taking my courage in my hands, I replied, 'I can prove to you that God exists by demonstrating it. But you will have to believe me. If you will trust my integrity, then I will give you the proof.'

We agreed, so I went on, 'You will be aware that I am looking for a house to buy so that I can bring my family here. You will also be aware that I have been out every evening viewing all the wallpaper in the county, but have found nothing. Now, God has told me to stop house-hunting, and he will show me the house. I believe that I shall see the house during this week. I'll keep you informed.'

Now I was on the spot. I looked at the diary. Today was Monday and, with the week effectively ending on Friday, there was no wiggle room in any timetable.

I waited. I had no idea what, if anything, might happen.

The hours slipped by and my life was surrounded by a crushing inactivity. Then, on Tuesday evening, as I was in my room and changing for dinner, there was a tap on the door. It was the porter.

'There is a gentleman on the lobby phone to speak to you.' He gave me a name which I did not know, but I hurriedly put on some shoes and walked briskly down to the ground floor foyer.

'Hello. Roy Peacock here.'

'Good evening. My name is Eric and you may not recall that we met briefly at an evening meeting in this area a couple of months ago.' This did not help me, but he continued.

'I'm not sure why I'm phoning you . . . it all seems rather silly to me . . . and I don't know in any case if this interests you. You see, I have a house for sale and, while I was praying about it, I felt the Lord tell me to let you know about it. I hope I'm not wasting your time.'

Wasting my time? I was almost crawling down the phone line with excitement. What could I say using a rational voice that didn't sound as if I had been breathing gas to make me squeak?

Trying to sound controlled, I responded rather slowly, 'Well, yes. As it happens we haven't yet made our arrangements. Could you tell me something about it?' As he spoke my heart fell. This was a piece of architectural history, one of the three largest houses on the town square in a local town. It had eight or nine bedrooms, the sitting room was just under forty feet long, the staircase, which had been removed from a medieval mansion in the town was recognized as from House Beautiful in Bunyan's *Pilgrim's Progress* – and the whole property, with copious outbuildings and stabling, stood in an acre of grounds. I didn't need to ask the price – I knew I could never afford it. Nevertheless, I did ask. My astonishment was then capped by frank amazement as the house price was adjusted, without any negotiation, to match what I could afford.

'Would you like to look at it?' Of course, but when? I had told my colleagues that I would see the house this week so, because I was driving home on Friday, it had to be Wednesday or Thursday.

Initially Eric preferred next week, and I resigned myself to missing my deadline. But after a few moments he said, 'I don't suppose you could make it for this Thursday.' I gulped.

'Yes, of course.'

'All right. Same arrangements, then, but this Thursday instead of next week.'

'Could I bring my wife with me?' I asked cautiously.

'Of course, I would expect you to do that.'

I telephoned home and, almost unable to speak in a rational voice, told Elizabeth that maybe the Lord was showing us our new home.

On Thursday Elizabeth and I drove to Eric's home. He lived in Ampthill in an environment of Georgian houses. The sun was shining, the front door was open and we were invited in and then straight along the hall to the open back door where we could see a patio on which was a white table with four chairs. We sat at the table and then saw that the one thing on it was an open Bible.

Eric explained, 'I've been praying about this and so have asked the Lord for a word in the matter. This is what he has given me. It is from the book of Esther, Chapter 4 and verse 14: "For if thou altogether holdest thy peace at this time, then . . . thou and thy father's house shall be destroyed: and who knoweth whether thou art come to the kingdom for such a time as this?" Roy, you will not be aware of this, but the house you are to see is not my house, but is jointly owned by me and my father-in-law.' He looked into the middle distance, then repeated to himself, 'Thou and thy father's house shall be destroyed . . . I think there is no doubt that it is in the mind of the Lord that you should have this house.'

And so we did.

# 6.

# At Home in Church

Elizabeth and I had been Christians for just a few weeks when we took a holiday, driving one of the vintage Rileys along the west coast of Somerset to Exmoor and beyond. This day became something of an epic since I had to strip and rebuild the car's braking system in a lay-by on the Somerset border – that is what made driving such an eventful affair!

Our first night away was spent in the village of Challacombe in North Devon in the western edge of Exmoor National Park. We learned that the local parish church was outside the village, and duly arrived at Holy Trinity Church on the Sunday morning with great anticipation. No one was there! As we walked back down the driveway, the congregation arrived in two or three cars and let us in. Being keen and new to it all, we took the pews at the front. The organist sat at his console, the man on the hand-pump rolled up his sleeves and we were under way as the organ grunted into life with what we took to be an introit. That finished, we sat around thinking fine thoughts until a lady approached us to say, 'The vicar has another church across the moor and we think he has been held up.' But when no vicar materialized she apologized that they would have to cancel the service.

As we walked to the door I ventured, 'Isn't it a pity when you think of it? We've all come to worship the Lord and, because one person hasn't arrived, we are all going home without doing so.'

'Well, since you put it like that, it is a shame, isn't it?'

Taking all of my courage into my hands, I pressed on. 'Why don't we have a service anyway? We could sing a couple of hymns, have a prayer . . .' here I paused, 'and if you like, I'll preach the sermon.'

The lady looked impressed. My wife was in shock.

The woman conferred quickly with her fellow members, rounded up the church warden who was already scurrying into the distance to get back to his cows, and before long it was all agreed.

We all strode back into the building, sat back down and the lady who did everything handed me a copy of *Hymns Ancient and Modern*, saying, 'Would you select the hymns for the organist, please?' I looked on in horror. I didn't know how the hymnbook was structured at all. Handing it back I said, 'I don't know your favourite hymns, so perhaps you could choose them.' Crisis averted, my next problem was what to preach on. At first I could not think of a single verse in the Bible, but then one popped into my mind. 'If ye then, being evil, know how to give good gifts unto your children: how much more shall your heavenly Father give the Holy Spirit to them that ask him?'

Whispering in a conspiratorial manner I asked Elizabeth where the verse was to be found. She knew! I turned to Luke 11:13, preached it and sat down before the vicar had time to walk in!

For the record, he never arrived, and as a final act I was asked to sign the service register. So the sixteenth-century parish church building of Challacombe bears the mark of my first sermon – and so, just maybe, do some of the congregation. To me it was a triumph. I had got myself into the most awful hole, the service had gone without a hitch and everyone seemed happy. There was just one thing I had forgotten, and that was to take up the offering!

Yet, without any knowledge at all of what the future held, or even if I would ever stand up to speak again, an international preaching ministry was born. Ours is not to know the future, but to advance one step at a time.

Upon our return from the holiday in Exmoor I had a phone call from a man who introduced himself as Gordon Penny. I had already discovered that, if there was any evangelistic work in the East Midlands, I could be sure to find the name of Gordon Penny in the small print. He was a remarkable man, always putting himself in the background but having, it seemed, immense positive influence on Christian work in the region.

'I hear that God has called you to a ministry of preaching.' I listened to him in incredulity. I'd never thought of preaching nor of the calling of God.

'Let me tell you what I'm going to do. I organize two Methodist circuits, one west of Derby and the other to the north. I'm going to put your name on the plan of both circuits so we can get you out preaching.'

In horror I responded, 'Wait a minute. I know nothing about preaching and I know nothing about Methodists.'

'Don't worry about that. I'll get John to go out with you.' So, like it or not – and I didn't much – I was now a preacher on two Methodist circuits. In due course, I met John and we arranged to meet near Foston, outside of Derby, for our first combined service.

The moment came. Together we prayed in the vestry and then walked up the steps to the pulpit where we sat, in a synchronized movement, at opposite ends on a long bench. It was two minutes to six by the clock strategically placed right in front of the preacher (to remind us of the shortness of life and the requirement that sermons be similar). Some music played in the background and at six o'clock precisely John rose to read what were known as Comfortable Words.

It was then that the first disaster of my budding preaching career transpired. John had been sitting at one extremity of the bench and I at the other. We had not noticed that the legs were some way in from the ends . . . so we were, in mechanical engineers' parlance, both cantilevers in balance with each other. As John rose with a most spiritual air, saying, 'Good evening, friends,' the bench was no longer in balance, so a watching, waiting world was treated to the remarkable sight of John rising above the sill of the pulpit while I quickly sank and disappeared from view.

It was a moment never to be forgotten . . . but so too was the sight a little later of over a third of the congregation giving their lives in prayer for a relationship with Jesus Christ.

Our disasters continued on a weekly basis, typically in Uttoxeter in a church building where the organ began a high pitched scream after the first verse of the first hymn. The organist issued his usual corrective by standing back and administering a sharp kick to the body of the machine. And so it went on. In the north of the county, the rather small congregation in a rather large building aligned themselves in the rear rows ready for a quick getaway. The exit door was surprisingly small and, as I watched, two men arrived at the exit from different directions. Both tried to be first out – and both got jammed in the doorway.

North of Derby in the Duffield area I spoke at one church with a plentiful but non-responsive congregation. At the close of the meeting I was approached by a little bent old man who whispered, 'Young man, for over thirty years I've prayed in this church every Sunday that I might one day hear the gospel of Jesus being preached. Today I heard it, in my church, for the first time.'

It had all been worthwhile.

Invitations began coming from different sources and, as the numbers grew, a diary took shape. This was to be a period when we learned of the scope of God's interest in our lives and his ambition to be involved in every part. To illustrate this I record just a few events, all involving people with whom, untypically for me, I have maintained contact over the years.

The beginning of every academic year involved seeing new faces and establishing new relationships. These were primarily at the academic level, but occasionally social. Paul Williams was one such. His earlier work in the aeronautical industry in Manchester had resulted in meeting John, a keen Christian who had now moved on to Cranfield where I had met him. In joining my department John arranged an introduction and we all finished up at my home talking about the things that aeronautical people talk about, then moving on to Christian matters. Paul realized that we were showing enthusiasm for all sorts of things that his denomination didn't involve itself in. As the evening drew to a close and we were about to pray, he broke his silence to say simply, 'I have a problem.' His problem, it transpired, was in smoking – he was a heavy smoker. His first act of the day, even before getting out of bed, was to have a cigarette.

John and I assured Paul that nothing was too difficult for God – even an addiction like his – and that, if he liked, we would pray for him to be set free. He liked, so we prayed.

The next morning, upon waking, Paul did not feel obliged to have his usual cigarette. This unexpected abstinence stayed with him until he went to the bus stop. The bus to Cranfield was a little late so, to while away the time, he decided to light up. Just then a bus drew up and, to his horror, the cigarette popped out of his mouth onto the pavement. Too embarrassed to pick it up again, he carefully trod on it as he climbed on board. He made his way to the upper deck, as was his custom, as this was a smoking area. It was a lengthy journey and so, to pass the time, Paul pulled out another cigarette. Once again the cigarette popped out of his mouth and fell to the floor.

What was going on? Then, as Paul now reports, he heard a voice within him, which simply said, 'You're under new management now.' That should have settled matters, but it didn't.

Back in his glass-walled office in Manchester, Paul's yearning for a 'ciggie' revived. But just as he went to light up he saw the door of the next office open, and who should walk in but John – one of those who had prayed for him at Cranfield. There was no way Paul could let John know that the smoking problem was not resolved, so he decided to hide the offending cigarette beneath the desk for the few moments that John was likely to be around. But John didn't go! He idled around the next-door office, while Paul's fingers got hotter as the cigarette slowly burned up, eventually burning his fingers as well.

Paul got the message. Today, forty years on, he still does not smoke.

Another student, Russell Heap, came from New Zealand to the United Kingdom to study and do research for a post-graduate degree in Aeronautical Sciences and spent a period on secondment with Rolls-Royce in Derby on his way to Cranfield. Russell was a Christian and it was therefore entirely natural that he would seek out other Christians working at Rolls-Royce. When he mentioned that he was going on to Cranfield to do some post-graduate work, he was warned to be careful in case he met a member of the faculty there called Roy Peacock. 'He's dangerous and to be avoided.' Russell noted the advice, filing it in the deeper recesses of his memory.

When he arrived at Cranfield Russell picked up a faculty list, only to find his memory being jogged when he saw my name. Matters were to get worse. As a major project he had opted to undertake the design of a small gas turbine engine to power a crop-spraying aircraft. The turbomachinery of the engine, being at the heart of the matter, meant that his supervisor would be the resident turbomachinist . . . Roy Peacock. Russell was duly alarmed.

The work advanced and we had several meetings. Although these began quite formally, they soon became more relaxed – which was just as well, for the day came when Russell arrived for his tutorial, limping badly, with his left foot in a trainer shoe. Naturally I was curious to know what he had been getting up to.

It transpired that Russell had been visiting a friend who lived in a caravan. Coming down the caravan steps he had slipped in icy conditions and wrenched his left knee badly, leaving him with ongoing, acute pain. His doctor had advised him that surgery may be necessary. We talked about what the Lord might do for him, and so it was that our usual concerns over increasing the thermal efficiency of an engine gave way to considering prayer for Russell's injury – hardly what a scientifically-based tutorial is usually about. When I told Russell that God was able to heal people's bodies, he asked if God might heal him. I had to say yes.

'When could he heal me?'

'Just any time,' I responded. I was nervous: it was getting to be like watching a car crash in slow motion.

'So . . .' Russell pressed on, 'could he heal me now?' I couldn't think of a way out of this impending disaster.

'Yes.'

'Could you pray for me?'

'When?' I croaked, my throat suddenly dry.

'Well, now of course.'

There was to be no getting away from this, so I came round to the front of my desk. I knew the Scripture, 'They shall lay hands on the sick and they shall recover' (Mark 16:18), so I knelt down to put my hand on his knee.

My office was at the end of a corridor which served only me and a rarely-used lecture theatre next door. The floor of this corridor was a heavy-duty lino which gave a clearly audible warning of potential visitors. It was at that very instant I heard such a warning! Immediately I recalled that I had arranged a tutorial for a student – a student now clearly on his way, about to knock on the door, stride in and see me kneeling in front of this man, hand on knee. The talk would be around the department in minutes, around the Institute within an hour and then things would move quickly. I would be summoned immediately to the Vice-Chancellor's office, where I would be invited to vacate the Institute immediately . . . although I would be promised that, so long as I didn't create any further embarrassment, the matter would be hushed up. My career would be over, all I had worked for finished, and my humiliation would know no bounds.

And so I stared disaster in the face.

Within my heart, I wanted to cry out to God. But what would I cry?

I heard the footfalls getting louder. When they reached the office door, the sound stopped. There was no knock, and the door didn't open. The silence was broken by the sound of footsteps receding down the corridor. And then they were gone. Why the student didn't enter, or even knock on the door, I will never know.

Suddenly I was free again – free to pray for my student, which I did.

The next day Russell could be seen without a limp and without a trainer on his left foot. I had to conclude that Russell has been healed.

It was a few years later that I was at the University of Pisa with Elizabeth and our daughter, Rachel. We were spending a few days in Tuscany and, in passing, visited the walled medieval town of Lucca. As we were crossing the central piazza I walked behind Rachel and Elizabeth. I was arrested by something about Rachel's walk: her toes were pointing in as she stepped forward.

Later on I asked about her feet and learned that she was walking on the outside of her feet to reduce the pain she had from verrucas. I knew nothing about verrucas, but I soon would. They are very contagious, and Rachel had picked up one, only to have it spread to the other foot.

Her doctor prescribed some cream to rub in – and the verrucas loved it! They grew vigorously. A series of progressively stronger creams had no effect at all, and eventually she was referred to a skin specialist. He was astonished at the gravity of the situation, saying there was little he could do. They had spread so far across her feet that the usual remedy of surgery was out of the question.

This was the situation when, one Sunday morning shortly afterwards, we went to church where I was speaking on 1 Corinthians. My address included a challenge to respond to a call from God for healing. Among those who came forward was a lady who, years before, had been caught in the London Blitz and had suffered raging tinnitus ever since. She was prayed for by members of the congregation and was instantly healed: her hearing returned to normal and the tinnitus had not returned when I saw her a year or so later.

Others came forward for prayer – including Rachel. Two ladies of the church prayed for her. Then we all went to our various homes for lunch.

That afternoon I exercised the preacher's prerogative by dropping asleep in an armchair, only to be awakened quite suddenly by screams from the top of the house where, two floors up, Rachel had a flat. I heard the noise of her feet thundering down the stairs. The rear hall door opened, followed quickly by the dining room door.

'Daddy, Daddy! Look at my feet!' So saying, she sat down, lifted both of her feet and showed me the soles. Other than two small verrucas, her feet were clear of any blemishes. And as we looked on, one of the last remaining verrucas curled up and fell off. The other was clear a few hours later.

Did it last? Was there any ongoing effect? We must flip over the pages of Rachel's and James's diary to discover the record.

James, her dance partner and later her husband, had been a keen dancer from his days at Oxford and Rachel began an interest in about 1998 at age 35. To make it to the top in this sport, it is necessary to begin dedicated training from an early age – some do so as early as four. There was, therefore, little chance of much real progress for Rachel, especially having had the foot problem with her crop of prize verrucas. In 2004 Rachel and James went to the dance championships at Blackpool, the famous dance venue in the north of England. Thinking that it would give them good experience, they decided to enter the Senior Ballroom Championship competition. That night, while I was in bed at 2 a.m., I was woken by the phone to hear my daughter's voice shouting in excitement. For a moment I thought she had crashed the car. But no. 'I'm in Blackpool. Daddy, we won at Blackpool. We won!' That stunning news – almost unheard of at the first attempt – was only the beginning. Recording only major competitions that Rachel and James have won over the years, a shortened list reads as follows:

Open English Senior Ballroom Champions 2006
South of France Senior Ballroom Champions 2006
World Senior II Ballroom Semi-Finalists 2008
Coupe De France Senior II Ballroom Champions 2010
Toulouse Grand Prix Senior Champions 2011

The ultimate accolade is in the fact that the English Senior Championship, the British Senior Championship and the UK Senior Championship were all won in the same two-year period, and in the World Championships they were listed as eleventh in the world. They are currently sponsored by a range of supporters who provide specially made dresses that would normally cost between £2000 and £3000 each (and which could sometimes end up on the BBC TV hit show *Strictly Come Dancing*), shoes, and James's tail suits. So their prowess is fully recognized.

As for me, I stand back in astonishment (and being the father, not a little pride) as I think of the girl, feet covered in verrucas, told that she should never expect to walk normally but always limp with pain. I think, 'That's my daughter.' Then I think again and say to myself, 'That's my God.'

One of the first physical miracles I ever saw concerned a lady whose legs were of differing lengths. As she was prayed for I watched as the short leg grew to match the other. Detractors may say that what was happening was no more than the spine and pelvis twisting to give the appearance of growth. To address this, I have always asked the person involved to sit back hard in a chair, thus precluding twisting. The lady concerned was the wife of a senior government scientist. After she was healed I watched her walk up the street, and couldn't help notice that she was not walking in a straight line, but progressing in a series of curves because of the new reach she enjoyed in her leg. That was forty-six years ago. We still have contact with this lady and the healing has been maintained.

To indicate that such miraculous activity is not a restricted thing, I mention that this sight has been replicated many times up to the present.

Maggie Manser is, by training, a nurse and has worked as a Nurse Practitioner. She is therefore ideally qualified to give a clear and objective account of her attendance at a meeting to which I was speaking locally on the 24th November 2009. I had made reference to the problem of odd-length legs, inviting people to respond to a call for healing. Maggie spoke to me at the end of the meeting, mentioning that, along with other members of her family, she suffered from odd-length legs. As a check, she seated herself and held her legs horizontally. Her right leg was one inch shorter than her left – a fact we confirmed quite simply by measuring the relative setting of the ankle bones. To relieve Maggie of the strain of holding her legs horizontally Rachel Sealey, a member of the congregation, held them for Maggie.

We prayed. Then things began to happen. A sudden pain in her left hip prompted Maggie to ask if I was praying for the correct leg. I thought so and told her which one. At this, the right leg began to move and grew half an inch.

Then it stopped. I checked the ankle joints and said, 'We need another half an inch, Lord.' And we got it! The two legs now matched and have done so ever since. Rachel felt the right leg growing in her hand and then watched as it moved to match the left leg. In her own words, as recorded on Facebook:

> Really excited last night during healing service at Harnhill. I had prayer for my R leg which was 1" shorter then L and painful for a while. Initially I had discomfort in my L hip but my R leg had grown 1/2". More prayer I could feel my R thigh bone growing longer!! Now no pain and legs equal length. How awesome and amazing is God. I can't stop thanking him and dancing on my new legs!

Why have I experienced such events? I don't know. All I have done is to try to honour the word of God and to hear his voice.

Meanwhile, the invitations to speak continued to come in. I was surprised to hear from the Apostolic Church, a denomination that had geographical areas of strength, especially in Wales where the work was born through the 1907 Welsh Revival. Would I be the main speaker at the World Annual Convention held, at the time, every year at the Pen-y-Groes Convention Centre in South Wales – and would I make a focus in speaking on the ministry of healing? I agreed.

I revelled in it. Every day there was a series of talks, sermons and exhortations of one sort or another. Possibly the finest preaching, on an ongoing basis, that I have ever heard. I could almost hear the mellifluous Welsh tones of Evan Roberts, Daniel Rowlands, Howell Harris, Christmas Evans, Seth Joshua and other historical figures of Welsh preaching.

And then I was asked to come forward. I stumbled through a few words, not even having the advantage of the correct accent, then made a challenge for folk to step out of their seats and come to the front for prayer. They filed out and I was astounded. I later learned that it was estimated one thousand people had responded.

But what should I do now? The president asked me to go into the audience to pray for people and to 'begin with the lady in the light green suit'. That was his wife. I had already learned that people being 'slain in the Spirit', falling over when they were prayed for, was frowned upon. So a circumspect approach was necessary.

I worked my way through the throng, found my target, stood in front of her and said,

'Give me your hands, my dear.' She did so, but before I could get into any meaningful prayer, she closed her eyes and, in what seemed like ecstasy, keeled over. I was horrified – what had I done? Then I looked around at the vast crowd and in astonishment saw dozens of people falling over as we prayed.

Was this what the Lord had in mind when he first called me in the Huntingdon fens, just outside of Cambridge? I don't know, but I was certainly fulfilled in what was happening.

Over the years I have sat under many sermons of one sort or another – some beautifully constructed and excellently presented and edifying. Yet from time to time I have felt rather disappointed by the lack of any effect on my life. Why was this? In time, I perceived a pattern. If the person of Jesus was central, if even his name was mentioned, there was a positive reaction in me. If not, I felt that something was missing. Clearly there was a correlation between a Christ-centred sermon and an inspired congregation. It became my determination, then, to preach 'Jesus Christ, and him crucified' (1 Corinthians 1:23; 2:2).

But what was the context to be for this preaching? It had to come from the Bible – that much was clear. Yet it also had to dig deep into my own life, and this became evident as the years unfolded.

The early days of our Christian lives were dominated by two features. One was the realization that the claims of the Christian faith were not pie in the sky but were valid and required an active response. The other was the anticipation of an ongoing conflict between my faith and my profession – both philosophically and in terms of a full diary. It has been rewarding to discover no such conflict.

When I had first arrived at Cambridge I had become fascinated by the subject of magneto-hydrodynamics, though my interest in the subject soon waned: I could see no potential application within the foreseeable future and, in any case, I had difficulty in spelling the word! And that underlined something in my own make-up – I wanted any work I did to have a practical benefit. This was to spill over into my Christian faith. I have only ever been interested in seeing its practical outworking and have never concerned myself with the more esoteric arguments. To use the old adage, I could not care less how many angels can stand on the head of a pin.

My research at Cambridge found its focus in viscous flows around bends – an inducement for most people's eyes to glaze over, but for me a fulfilment which I would have described as 'what life is all about'. After about two years of design and experiment, I had to consider earning a living to look after my family. We had, by now, learned to live a very low-cost life, having abandoned good food, all drink but tea (builders brew!) and only ate meat once a fortnight. We discovered a particularly cheap cut of lamb called breast of lamb – a cause for some celebration until the day Elizabeth overheard a woman in the butcher's reel off a mouth-watering order which finished up with, 'Oh, and I'll have a breast of lamb please – it's for the dog.' Breast of lamb never tasted the same again!

In one job interview I met the Chief Scientist at Rolls-Royce, Steve Bragg, and his Chief Engineer, Stan Smith. I was soon being interrogated gently by a pair of sharp minds.

'Is the phenomenon you are researching of importance?'

'Oh, yes. And it's very interesting.'

'I'm sure. But what is the effect on the performance of the compressor of an aero-engine?' I had no idea, never having thought about it, so I made a guess.

'It reduces the performance.'

'Yes, of course. But by how much? What is the loss of performance?'

I had no idea whatsoever but I knew that to say so was to be invited to close the door as I left the room. By now, I was in a blue funk, groping for an answer – anything that didn't sound too stupid. Through a strangely dry throat I croaked, 'In normal operation for a modern aero-engine, you have sacrificed 2% in efficiency due to this phenomenon.'

The office fell into silence as these two powerful men considered their position. A lot was at stake – the budget they oversaw was considerable, running into millions.

'That's very interesting,' said Steve Bragg, 'That is exactly the number that we have assessed it to be. How did you get it – and so precisely?'

'Well, actually, that is what my work is about, and in doing the research and taking the measurements, a fellow builds up an understanding.' That was coded language to say I'd guessed.

'We are impressed.' I heard the words through a fog. 'But tell us how you get rid of this problem.'

I tried to sound authoritative as I laid out the options I would explore.

'Right then. How would you like to do that and then tell Rolls-Royce how to manage this problem? We would like you to join the company, though we think it would be beneficial if you stayed at Cambridge where you have your research facility and do the work there. You would be directly answerable to Steve here.'

I returned to my laboratory with a light heart.

These were happy, fulfilling days with an agreeable pattern of life – a fast drive in my vintage Riley to the laboratory, a quick look at the morning mail, then to the top floor of the building where I could sit in isolation and fiddle with the sums that might change the world. Come lunch-time a quick trip to the Granta, a pub on the River Cam just away from the city centre, after which the day continued, punctuated by tea and sticky buns at four, before the working day ended around eight. Nothing could be better organized than that and nothing could disturb it. Or so I thought. But I hadn't accounted for the changed life that resulted from becoming a Christian.

Nor had I thought of the consequences of inviting people into our home to learn of the Christian message.

As we began to realize what this new life had to offer, we wanted others to know about it. We had asked David (he of the big boots) how we might go about this. At first he seemed at a loss, but he did say that we might start a Bible study in our home. Now that was a great but potentially short-lived idea when we realized that neither of us knew anything about the Bible – I would often explain to people that I didn't even know who the prophet Genesis was. David came to the rescue: he had read the Bible, therefore we were confident that he could answer all our questions. (Years later he revealed that, all the time we were taxing him with questions, he felt he was never more than five minutes ahead of us.) So who should we ask to join us?

'You don't ask anybody. You simply pray and God will bring them in.'

The man was quite mad, of course . . . but then, he had been right about the Christian life – maybe, just maybe, he was right about this. So we prayed and within a week five people had approached us and asked if they could come to the Bible study. We were agog.

They came. Each week, under David's instruction, we prayed specifically for one person. Then we watched as, the following week, that person would be changed fundamentally. Michael was soon in full time service, working with an itinerant evangelistic mission where he quickly took on Bible teaching duties, a clear call on his life. Muriel, his wife, joined him. Margot made a commitment, and so did Kenneth. In the end just one person would fall by the wayside, but for the others this was to be a lifelong dedication to Jesus Christ.

We moved to Derby and then on to Bedfordshire as my work demanded. Would this be the end of such meetings?

On our first Thursday evening at our new home in Bedfordshire we were surprised to hear a ring at the front door. 'We've come to have fellowship with you.' Three men stood there, announcing themselves as Jeeves, Lamb and Houfe. Two were complete strangers, and I felt like Abraham standing in the door of his tent (Genesis 18). So I invited them in and our conversation turned immediately to the things of the Lord.

Although quiet and retiring in their demeanour, these men had testimonies to send a listener's head reeling. Lamb, for instance, had fought in the First World War. While in the trenches his unit often came under direct fire. When that happened, all the men in the unit would crowd up close to him, declaring that he was a man of God and God would not allow him to be killed – so their best chance of living was to stick close to him! Lamb's presence with us indicated one thing in particular – they had been right.

Elizabeth and I weren't sure about what was happening. Imagine our astonishment when, on the next Thursday evening, the door-bell rang to reveal half a dozen people. We talked about the things of God and read a little of the Bible together before we concluded in prayer. What on earth was happening? None of these people had been invited. But the following Thursday evening even more came. And so it went on, as we went off to buy stacking chairs to accommodate the Thursday-nighters. The maximum number we had at a meeting was 140, none of whom we had invited but all of whom were hungry to meet God.

The meetings ran for over ten years and I have no idea how many people came, but I can confidently say that it was in the thousands. Unbeknown to us, the drawing room on the first floor of our house where the meetings were held became known as the Upper Room. It was there that we saw many lives changed. In later years, when I was involved in ministry globally, I was hugely encouraged to meet several folk, from time to time, who had had a vital experience with God 'in a place called the Upper Room in Ampthill in England'.

Among those early visitors was a lady who announced herself memorably when she first appeared at the door: 'Praise the Lord, I'm a Pentecostal!' She was Italian, outgoing and exuberant; we were frightened! But her vital expressiveness soon brought a reward.

Anne was an acquaintance of Elizabeth, a very quiet, rather introspective lady who arrived just as the meeting began and went to the one seat she could find easily. It was next to the Italian lady.

The evening progressed quietly until the forty or so people present turned to prayer. At this point Anna, our Italian, began beseeching the Lord to intervene in a situation which, so far as I could work out, involved her brother. She was now moving into top gear, her voice rising with accompanying cries of anguish. She was evidently finding her English wasn't up to the occasion, as her language changed – either to her native Italian or perhaps another tongue altogether. Whatever it was, she meant it. When she finally came to a halt, no one knew quite what to do.

The silence was broken by a small voice. 'Thank you, God, for bringing me here.' It was Anne. Within a few minutes she had given her life to the Lord and was transformed by a faith that has proved life-saving in grave personal difficulties over the many years since.

Of the innumerable visitors we had, few could have had such an effect as the brother of one of our regular visitors. She telephoned one Thursday evening before the meeting, clearly in torment. Her brother had travelled from the other side of Europe, leaving behind his wife and his girlfriend to decide between them. He had chosen the latter. He was now, as we spoke, on his way to Heathrow Airport to get a flight to see her. Would we pray?

Soon people began arriving for the meeting and we began as usual with prayer and singing. At about 8.15 p.m. I heard a noise on the staircase and, thinking that one of my children was out of bed, went to attend to matters. There I encountered a man I had never seen before, behind whom stood our regular visitor who had telephoned earlier. He was led into the praying roomful of folk. Now, nobody knew who he was or anything about him, but he had been seated just a few minutes when someone spoke a word that was quite clearly from God. 'I know where you are,' he began. 'You knew me once but you have not followed me, yet I have not let you go. I have attached to you a silken cord which cannot be broken and I have followed you. But tonight I am drawing the cord in, to take you to myself. You are mine, says the Lord.'

As the speaker finished, someone next to him picked up the theme and continued the prophecy. And so it went on across half a dozen people or so. I was stunned – but so, evidently, was the subject of God's interest. After a few more minutes someone came to whisper in my ear that the visitor wanted to speak to me in private.

We went to a quiet room where he poured out his heart. I suggested that we should pray. After a few moments he said he could feel a wind blowing. Oh dear, I thought. I knew that we lived in a large old house full of draughts and leaking windows, but I had to admit that I had never known a draught in this room. But he continued. 'And now, as well as the wind, I can hear a fire crackling here. It's crackling all around me.' It was only then that I realized that the Holy Spirit was manifesting himself in a scriptural pattern to this man, even though I could not hear it.

Needless to say, the Lord had the man's attention, and his flight from Heathrow was abandoned.

Not everyone who came to the meetings was healed. Jon was a regular. He had cerebral palsy and came, week by week, in a wheelchair, bent over with his two arms held tightly to his side, hands always clenched. He was carried upstairs into the drawing room where we often prayed for him. One evening several of us felt that we should pray for his healing. In a crowded room filled with praying support-ers we watched with growing amazement as Jon lifted his right hand from its permanent position. He opened his hand, flexed his fingers and stretched them in freedom. The roomful of people was exultant: Jon was being healed and would, we were sure, step out of his wheelchair and be a tremendous testimony.

But it was not to be. As Jon looked in amazement at his raised hand his face began to cloud over. Then, to our dismay, he snatched his hand back to his body and folded it in its normal position with the arm pressed against his rib-cage.

What was I going through at this time? It seems to me now that it was a kind of apprenticeship. Just as I had learned to do metalwork and to master detailed engineering drawings for five years, so that I might ultimately become a competent worker in my field of fluid mechanics, so those early days in the Upper Room were a spiritual apprenticeship where I was shaped by God to become, as Paul puts it, an able minister of the New Testament (see 2 Corinthians 3:6).

One evening Eric, a celebrated architect, began chatting to us. 'You know, Roy, Jeeves and Lamb and I used to meet weekly to pray for this area. We prayed, "Lord God, please send us a man." We did this every week for over thirty years and then . . .' – at this point Eric looked me straight in the eye – '. . . I met you. Immediately after that I phoned the men and said, "I've just met the man God has sent in answer to our prayers." '

It was a moment to stand in awe of God and make a dedication to whatever he had in mind for us.

The startling and unpremeditated events at Holy Trinity in Challacombe in northern Exmoor were not my first challenge in Christian speaking. That occurred in Hemingford Grey when, a few weeks after becoming Christians,

Elizabeth and I were invited to contribute to a short series of testimonies of people in the village who had been touched by the recent week of evangelism. Four of us would tell our stories for a few minutes each in the quietness of a living room – not before an enquiring audience but for a tape recorder. For me, I assessed, this would be simple. When I made presentations of my scientific work, principally in Cambridge, I could hold the interest of a critical audience. So, I decided: same method, different message.

For me, Cambridge had been the school of hard knocks. There I could expect an unforgiving and critical audience made up of specialists who wanted to assert themselves and destroy the speaker. I recalled having been invited to give a seminar on my research before an audience of a formidable array of university professors, supported by my own peers who were all learning to survive in such a competitive environment. Nervous at first, I gained composure as my audience listened intently – and then disaster struck.

One professor (my boss) was a world authority on fluid mechanics and secondary distributed vorticity in particular, and a Fellow of the Royal Society (the most prestigious scientific institution in the world). He interrupted to ask a question about the graph I had on the screen. I answered briefly and made to carry on, but he stopped me and returned to his question. In fact he had found a chink in my armour and in the space of a few moments destroyed me verbally. I limped to the conclusion of my presentation and then, ashamed, fled for the sanctuary of my office.

And I thought: never, but never again, would I put myself in the position where my arguments would not be thought through beforehand and I could not make a good hand of defending myself.

So, with such a background, and now with an invitation to present my testimony for posterity, I could feel comfort in the thought, 'Same method, different message.' I was, however, blissfully unaware of the ultimate support on offer to the Christian. It is a promise that the Holy Spirit can guide us and I was to learn that this claimed guidance could become a vital feature of my Christian life. A parallel to this is the guidance given by a trained dog for blind people and, certainly, I had yet to have my eyes opened to this as a living experience.

We agreed a batting order. Muriel, a local lady, spoke first, movingly describing her meeting with the Lord. Michael followed. Elizabeth was engaging as always. And then it was my turn. I knew just what to do. I had rehearsed the first sentence – from there it would roll. And, sure enough, out came the first sentence. Then, with my attentive audience of four before me, I froze . . . not a thought, not a word, nothing. I didn't know what to say or how to say it. There was some harrumphing and then a torrent of unrelated words and phrases poured out, to the embarrassment of all. I later learned that mine was the only track that needed editing.

It was a couple or so weeks later that we were encouraged to go to a meeting in a house in St Ives, Huntingdonshire, to hear a speaker. Elizabeth clearly went with anticipation, whereas I was still licking my wounds. Before we set off, I had prayed and become convinced that this would be a signal day in my life. When we arrived we found seats in a large but crowded sitting room where I could see beyond the speaker to a window and the view outside. Settling down, I was astonished to see a white dove flying to and fro outside. Now, I'm not one to be ever on the look-out for signs, but I was well aware that the Bible speaks of the Holy Spirit in a form like a dove.

I took it as a portent. Before we left, I was to be found kneeling in a bedroom in prayer and having the most amazing experience with God – one that defies description. I was on holy ground.

From that time, Christian speaking assumed a new dimension for me. I didn't need to apologize for introducing Jesus into a conversation, and I could safely anticipate that he would be as good as his word in any situation. Further, rather than apologizing for the Bible giving misleading information, I began to understand that I could rely on it and see it being worked out. After all, my shelves of reference books, archive papers and scientific reports had certainly eased my way through my scientific life; so now I was discovering that the Bible had a purpose.

And it wasn't to press flowers or act as a door-stop.

# 7

# God Is Still Speaking

God speaks to his people. This fact is part of the armoury of the Holy Spirit, and it underpins all that I have recorded in this book. Sometimes God speaks through what is called 'the word of knowledge' (1 Corinthians 12:8). For reasons that are beyond my understanding this is something normally ignored or even discouraged within the church. In fact we have replaced this direct relational activity with God by various layers of oversight, called by a variety of names across the denominations but all equally capable of stifling the work of the Spirit. So we have elders, pastors, vicars, rectors, bishops, archbishops, fathers – the list is endless – all of whom of course have a contribution to make within the life of the church, but none of whom have the right to deny or replace the one-to-one relationship with God that is the spiritual birthright of every believer.

Towards the end of the last century there grew up denominational structures that were fashioned around a form of oversight known as shepherding. Doctrinaire and controlling, it brought power and prestige to the shepherds, but prison to the sheep. Here the sheep neither needed to hear from God nor were expected to; their shepherd did the hard work of listening before handing down the word of God, which was then to be obeyed. I was so disturbed by this fundamental departure from biblical Christianity that I wrote a book, *The Shepherd and the Shepherds*, which exposed this fallacious teaching. I was roundly condemned for breaking rank and telling all.

I must say, with passion, that the word of God is precious, personal and pertinent. It speaks directly into situations. It can be relied upon. And it will glorify God. Though many Christians remain unaware that God has reserved this fundamental feature of life for them, the truth remains that we can all discover that God speaks to his people. In fact, we may find him to be rather talkative!

So what was the purpose behind that time-consuming and, frankly, challenging series of events leading to our change of home from Derby to Bedfordshire? As is often the case, it is only in retrospect that I can see why this occurred.

Every step that we took required two things: a word from God and faith in our response. As we came to see that the word from God was to be trusted, it took on a more vital place within our lives. As we exercised faith – a specific trust, not just the general kind of 'Christian faith' that makes up our belief system – so we became spiritually alive. This kind of faith was an active part of living, more like breathing: if you don't breathe, you don't live. No wonder an inspired writer recorded that 'whatsoever is not of faith is sin' (Romans 14:23).

This was a foundation for our Christian lives, hammered into us by day-to-day experience. The twofold essentials of our lives were (and are) the word of God and the faith to see it put into practice. Whenever I was asked what the

Christian life was all about, I would respond with just those words.

So what do I mean when I say that God speaks to a person? We have seen that, right back at the beginning as recorded in Genesis Chapter 1, God spoke. Throughout the Old Testament God speaks to a large number of people. It seems to be in his nature to communicate. And if he spoke throughout history, we may conclude that as an unchanging God (that's his claim!) he speaks right now.

But how does God speak? Here we need to be more circumspect, for this is a matter for him to decide. In those hours immediately before my conversion, I had the privilege of hearing God speak – audibly. But that was just once. In general, I have found the Lord speak to me through highlighting a word while I am in prayer or reading my Bible or even some other book. Then again, it may be through a word from a friend or colleague. But, whichever way it comes, I look for confirmation via other means, so that I may be sure this is from the Holy Spirit.

This can be an exciting avenue of ministry, although sadly not without its discouragements along the way. I was speaking to a group of Christians in the South-East of England when it seemed that God was speaking to me about the illness of someone present. I spoke the word to the congregation but there was no response. I carried on. At the end of the service I was approached by the leader who asked if anyone had responded, though he already knew the answer. 'If there was no response,' he said, 'then the word was false. You were wrong and God did not speak to you, so your whole presentation to this assembly was a false one.' I was crushed. I was new to all this and had no answer at all.

It took me some time to recover. Later, I had an engagement in the village of Bentley just outside Ipswich. Here I spoke two words: one for a person who suffered from debilitating migraines; and the other for a woman with a lump in the breast. Again, no response. What was going on?

After this I spent a period in Canada where I was very cautious about speaking any words from God, and I have to say there seemed to be little benefit from the tour. Returning to England, I found myself back near Ipswich. I was standing close to the door as people came in, when a man came over to speak to me.

'I wonder if you recall coming here about three months ago?' Did I recall it? It seemed as if my walk with God had fallen apart since then. As I tried to answer him, I broke down in tears – much to his embarrassment. He pressed on. Did I remember two words of knowledge I had had, one regarding terrible migraine attacks and the other concerning a woman with a lump in the breast? I nodded, unable to speak. 'I think you should know,' he continued, 'that I was the migraine sufferer. I didn't respond at the time since I wasn't sure if God had healed me, but I have never had a migraine since. I have been healed!

'Incidentally,' he continued, 'my wife didn't respond either, but she was the woman with the lump in the breast. It was cancer. When we got home she examined her breast and the lump was gone. She was healed as well!'

And then he added firmly, 'You should know this.'

About eight years ago I was part of the congregation in a church in Combe Down near Bath, when we were intro-

duced to a visiting family whose daughter was doing missionary work in Paraguay. The church was invited to pray for
her. I knew (and still know) nothing about Paraguay other
than that it is in South America – somewhere in the middle.
The fact that it had not been in the news suggested to me
that it was a stable nation.

As the church prayed for her, I was astonished to see a
vision of a tree, fully formed and standing some twenty-
five feet tall, in leaf. The leaves were bright red, all pointing
upwards and flickering in the sunlight. And then I realized
that I was not looking at leaves at all – these were actually
flames covering the tree. As I watched, the tree began to
topple and then fall over, but the myriad of little flames
continued to burn. Then they fell off and spread around the
tree, rushing outwards from the main trunk.

I had never seen anything like it before (or since!), but I
walked across to the missionary and told her what I could see
and, by way of interpretation, I said, 'The tree is the nation of
Paraguay. The time will come when the nation enters political strife and revolution, but the flames emanating from the
trunk are lights of the gospel. You will see problems occurring
in the nation but this is the prelude to a work of God there.'

The girl looked at me carefully and asked, 'Did you know
that an outstanding characteristic of Paraguay is the trees
that grow across the nation? They have bright red foliage
and they're known as flame trees.'

I could not have been more thrilled, and we all recognized
the vision to have come from God.

About a year later the church was visited by a couple who,
it transpired, were also from Paraguay. After they had shared

the story of their work I decided to share what I had said to the girl the year before. Their reaction was quite different: clearly thinking I was mad, they rather quickly finished the conversation and went to talk to someone – anyone! – who was on hand.

Of course I was disappointed, but I wrote the whole matter off to experience. That is, until I read some years later that the President of Paraguay, Fernando Lugu, had in fact been deposed in a coup. I regard this not as an amusing sideline in Christian storytelling, but as a clear indicator that the word of God is never abstract or empty of application. We disregard the word of knowledge at our peril.

The encouragement that I did have in those earliest of days was from reading the Bible. The word I read was a lamp for my feet and a light for my path. It was a word I could rely upon – though when someone suggested that the Bible – and that alone – was all I needed to live the Christian life, I did wonder whether I even needed to pray! But of course the Bible is to be read within the context of a personal relationship with the living God.

During this period, as I strove to see a consistency in all I was taught, I came to understand that the heroes of the Bible – be they patriarchs, prophets, or priests – were all human beings, like me. However, before I became open to the living word of the Lord, their experiences seemed to have no parallels with mine, even though we shared a similar belief in God. It was George Whitefield who illuminated this level playing field to which we are all brought, when he said, 'The best of men is but a man, at best.'

I prayed about the matter. The substance of my prayer was, 'Lord, I am reading about all these people who had a relationship with you. Time and time again I read that the Lord spoke to Moses, the Lord spoke to Elijah, the Lord spoke to Elisha, to Abraham, to Isaac, to David . . . in fact it seems to me that the Lord spoke to just about everybody. But, Lord, I can't say that you have ever spoken to me. Yet I believe that this Christian life you have given me is not lacking in any way. I don't see different grades of Christian in the Bible – those who are privileged to hear from God and those who are not. Why is it that you don't speak to me? Are we living in a different age where your methods have changed? Why don't you speak to me?'

As I sat quietly in prayer, to my total astonishment, a complete answer popped into my heart, and I heard it in awe.

'I am the Lord. I change not. I am the same for ever and ever. I do now what I did then and have done throughout history. I speak to you in precisely the same way as I spoke to your forefathers, to the patriarchs and to all those recorded in my word. I am the Lord. I change not.'

I thought this through before daring to respond. 'But Lord, what is the difference between these people and me?'

'They heard the word. They received the word. And they obeyed the word.'

Now I could see that the dialogue deficit was not in God – it was in me! If the source of the problem could be identified in me, then it was close enough to be dealt with by me. And this resulted in a dedication on my part: that I would seek to listen to God and then be obedient to him.

Now, it is fair to ask, 'What does God say?' If he speaks, is it ever relevant to the details of my life, or should I expect to hear generalities only – those things that provide a foundation for my Christian life but where I carry the responsibility of interpreting the word and matching it up to my particular situation? When the voice in the cave asks, 'What doest thou here, Elijah?' (1 Kings 19:9) is this really the word of God for me at this moment or, if I seek to apply it directly to my current situation, am I simply indulging a fertile mind? Did Elijah even hear anything, or was he undergoing some kind of hallucination or breakdown? Or, finally, was this merely a good storyline?

A lot can depend on addressing these questions properly and getting the answers right.

Over the years God has gone on graciously speaking to me – even when I have not been aware of it straight away.

I had been invited to speak at a Ladies Conference in Dorset. As an enjoyable day drew to a close one of the organizers asked me to go with her husband and speak to one of the delegates who had gone on home.

We arrived at the place and the doorbell was answered by a welcoming lady who introduced herself as 'Jane . . . Calamity Jane. That's the story of my life,' she said, 'and it's why I wanted to talk to you.' She also mentioned that she thought her house was spiritually influenced and would value prayer for that as well.

After further conversation, we bowed our heads and waited on the Lord. To my considerable astonishment, he gave me a vision. I was at some height above an oily-looking sea, the swell unbroken by waves. As I watched from a height of about a hundred feet, I noticed a disturbance in the water beneath me. This continued and grew until the surface was broken by something emerging from the depths below. As it rose from the water, I saw that it was a steel, open-work cradle of considerable size, painted bright yellow. Lying in the bottom of the cradle was a black, slimy object which defied accurate description.

The picture went and was replaced by another.

I was now at sea level, looking over the surface of a choppy sea, waves creaming at their tops, the sea beneath a deep marine blue. Across the surface of the water there came a three-masted sailing ship, looking majestic as it ran before the wind, sails filled, the bow making an impressive foam track across the ocean.

In my heart, I said, 'Lord, what on earth am I looking at? It doesn't make sense to me.' Then he spoke to me and, as he did, I recognized it from years before. 'This,' said the Lord, 'is the Mary Rose. You saw it after it had sunk in the Solent and was being raised from its grave. But now you have seen my intention for this girl. I will raise her from the depth of her past and I will restore her – even as you know the Mary Rose is being restored. And then she will sail in my glory, blown by the wind of my Spirit. This is my word for her.'

Now, I have to admit to being very cautious over matters like this, and I worry that I might declare something to be the word of the Lord when it isn't. Confirmation is what I always look for, but on this occasion I knew that I must act without that and move ahead solely in faith. How on earth could we ever know whether this was from God or perhaps just a figment of an active imagination? But, feeling a weight of responsibility, I gave the word.

The woman heard me, listening carefully, then said slowly, 'Do you remember how I met you at the door and introduced myself?'

'I do. You said that your name is Jane, Calamity Jane, and that is your problem.'

'That's right,' she said. 'But what I didn't tell you was this. Everybody knows me as Jane, but that's not actually the name on my birth certificate. My real name – which no one knows – is Mary Rose.'

The rest of God's word for her is, I understand, still being worked out. It does take a little while to build a ship.

# 8.

# A Pair of Working Boots

There are plenty of Christian books around. The range is enormous – theology, apologetics, teaching, aids to prayer, aids to worship, biblical exposition, biographies and autobiographies abounding. Possibly because they make for easy reading, biographies and testimonies are particularly popular, and they can certainly be faith-building.

So it was for me. I devoured the exciting accounts of missionaries in faraway places; I was encouraged by heart-warming accounts of family life lived under the hand of God; I was built up as I read of the triumph of those living as Christians in an alien society. But the fact is that I had not been to these faraway places; my family life didn't go through the same set of crises; I was not planning on living in an area where, as a Christian, I might be in danger. By contrast my life was contained within a rather small envelope: office and laboratory by day, home every evening and morning, and church at some point over the weekend.

Exciting and uplifting as these books were then, this raft of literature didn't directly apply to my life. I was not a zealous Christian with a pith helmet, nor a housewife facing the pressures of bringing up a family, nor even someone given to dissecting the theology behind what I was reading in my Bible. I was a scientist, immersed in applying thermodynamics, as I developed an engineering research laboratory.

In consequence, as time passed, I was inadvertently developing two parallel lives: the spiritual, which was expressed on Sundays with a 'topping up' during the week at mid-week meetings; and the secular, which was expressed mainly at work. In fact, I do not recall ever listening to a church sermon expressly challenging me to expect God to intervene in my working life.

At a discussion in the City of London one businessman put it this way: 'I express my Christian life over the weekend when I go to church and engage in numerous Christian activities with my family. But then, on Monday morning, I return to my professional responsibilities at the office and leave my Christianity on the doormat as I go in.'

He was not alone. This was my lifestyle and that of many others – encouraged, frankly, by the teaching given to us at church. It was put to us, quite forcibly, that secular work was the devil's domain; but, in a modern world, it had to be done to put food on the table (and money for the tithe, which seemed to be the subliminal message).

It was an unspoken corollary that success in one's working life was rather frowned upon: such effort should be reserved for the Lord's work. On one occasion (unconnected with that particular church), when I had taken up the editorship of a Christian journal, I received a letter from a person who had thought, incorrectly, that this editorial job had involved resignation from my scientific endeavours. He congratulated me for having left all that behind to dedicate myself to the things of God. We entered a correspondence in which he told me that he had been registered to study for a PhD in his scientific discipline, when the elders of his church put him right on the issue. He had therefore abandoned his studies, resigned his registration and was now 'doing the Lord's work'.

And so my life was sharply partitioned between the spiritual on one side and the carnal on the other, each side developing independently as time went by.

But that was to change.

One of the pleasures of my life after becoming a Christian had been to attend evangelistic meetings – especially, as things worked out, the sort held in large tents. Unless I was standing in damp grass or sitting on an uncomfortable folding chair, with a chill wind blowing through a crack in the canvas, and the music coming through an electronic organ attended by out-of-tune guitars, it simply was not the gospel. And this was one of those evenings.

The evangelist knew success in his ministry. Starting out some years before with a circular tent comprising two 'D' shaped segments, the need had grown to insert a parallel section, then another and another. Eventually, the tent had grown into a long tube. At one end the evangelist stood on stage, while I was sitting at the other end. As always, his speaking was persuasive, although at that distance some concentration was needed so that nothing was lost.

That was exactly the situation when I was startled to hear the Lord speak inside of me. This was nothing directly to do with the subject of the evening, so the content of what he said was even more surprising. 'You've never given me all of your life,' he said. Now that was quite a challenge to someone who felt a strong dedication to the things of God.

'But I have, Lord,' was my indignant response.

'You've never given me all of your life.' The word was insistent and, in my normal manner, I was prepared to argue the point.

'I remember when I gave my life to you and I became a Christian. I didn't try to hold anything back. I've given you my life.'

Again, the convicting word came, 'You've never given me all of your life.'

At this point, I challenged God, 'Tell me: what haven't I given to you?' It was in astonishment that I heard the Lord say, 'You've never given me all of your work. You've never given me your research.' That much was true, but then it was too small a matter to concern the Lord, as I explained to him. 'My research programme involves one small experimental rig and one student. That's all.'

'Give that to me.'

Reluctantly, I did.

But what did that mean? I wasn't sure, but I thought I might start by praying when I got into the office every morning. To be honest, it seemed odd. Fortunately my office had a satisfyingly thick wooden door and frosted windows. I prayed on through my embarrassment, asking the Lord to take over all the work I would be doing that day.

The main focus of my programme at that time was in writing a scientific paper, a process that would absorb several weeks. Now, there are certain protocols to be observed for such a paper to be acceptable, not least the matter of referencing and cross-referencing. If a piece of work depended upon some earlier work for its provenance, an author would list that work at the end of his paper. The author should always be careful to do that, since an omission is regarded as rather bad form.

The paper I was writing concerned a three-dimensional gas flow problem which, in the world of fluid mechanics, tends to be a little complex in its mathematics. I had reached the point where I needed to find an appropriate foundational reference, but I realized that the phenomenon was so well known that I had never previously bothered to refer to any seminal work. What could I do here? Nothing came to mind and I was stuck.

It dawned on me that if I believed that God might be disposed to help me, then he could lead me to my reference. Perhaps I should pray.

I did. And I waited. Oh well, it was worth a chance, but that was that.

A few minutes later I received a telephone call from a colleague. Could I swop lecture slots with him the following week? I could and said I would go to his office to finalize the arrangements. I tapped on his door and walked in. Ken was a very short man who kept his office piled high with untidy columns of papers. His domain proclaimed that nature abhors a vacuum – and Ken certainly did. Although I couldn't see him, I knew that he was there as I could hear his voice on the phone coming from behind the paper mountain on his desk.

The telephone conversation continued as I stood waiting. I glanced idly at the table to my left, piled with papers in the familiar way, and I noticed one pile, neater than the rest, consisting of archive papers issued by the American Institute of Aeronautics and Astronautics. About one third of the way down one report stuck out from the pile. Checking that Ken was still occupied, I slid it out from the others to read the title on the cover. This led to me feverishly speeding through the entire document as I realized that here, in my hands, was the very piece of information I had been praying for.

I was stunned. When Ken and I had finished I returned to my office in triumph. The prayer appeared to have been answered. Was this a co-incidence, perhaps? I couldn't resist a quick statistical analysis. Running a few numbers through my head, I soon realized that the probability of this happening was remote.

In my hands, I concluded, was an answer to prayer.

Much of my scientific work has taken me abroad over the years, so flying has become a routine part of life. When I first began commercial airlines did not have quite the competitive edge with which we have since become familiar. I soon discovered that trans-Atlantic traffic followed a tidal pattern, flights tending to be full at weekends, while mid-week flights were often quite empty. Airlines made every attempt to sell surplus seats on the day of the flight at knock-down prices.

Here was a system I could play. Over the week before my crossing I would call the three main carriers daily to find out the percentage of seats sold. Tuesdays to Thursdays the flights would often be about half full, so I could be sure to purchase a seat at the airport immediately before checking in – at a fraction of the normal ticket price.

That was fine until it all went wrong.

During that time I was due to speak at the next in a series of weekly meetings in Seaside, California. So far the meetings had gone well, the congregation growing to a full-capacity crowd of eight hundred.

I arrived at Heathrow close to the PanAm desk, wandered in and said airily to the ticketing clerk, 'A ticket for this morning's flight to Los Angeles – one of the cheap ones at sixty pounds, please.'

'Sorry, sir. The flight is full.'

'What?' I exclaimed. 'I mean today's flight to LA – it leaves in about forty minutes.'

'As I said, the flight is full, sir.'

'But it can't be!' By now I was alarmed. 'It was only half full yesterday.'

'And it's full today, sir.'

Panic set in. There were no further flights that day on any of the main carriers, so I had to settle for any city on the West Coast – any flight, any seat. And so it was that I came to a departure lounge packed, shoulder to shoulder, with hundreds of other passengers, all going to San Francisco. I stood there for a few minutes as boarding got under way. I glanced around, wondering what it would be like to share a lifeboat with these folk, and then mused that I didn't really need to worry – Boeing 747s didn't have lifeboats!

As I looked around, my eye caught the most unpleasant looking man I could imagine. He gave a new definition to 'fat'. Dressed from head to foot in a black polo neck sweater and matching black trousers, he had a large, bushy, white beard. He looked like a cross between Father Christmas, King Kong and the Michelin man. With him was a tiny and insignificant-looking lady. It was a good job that this was a big aeroplane and I was unlikely to see them on the flight.

I waited for the usual scramble for seats (that were allocated anyway) to die down, and then wandered down the aisle until, horror of horrors, I saw the empty seat. It was one of a row of three, the other two occupied by King Kong and his wife!

Standing in the aisle, I said, 'Excuse me. I think that that must be my seat.' This was greeted by a malevolent stare from the gorilla man and a resigned look from his wife as they let me take my window seat.

The lady decided that she would read, as the flight was so long, but after a few minutes of increasing panic rummaging about in her bag, she exclaimed, 'Oh dear, oh dear! I think I left my book in the hotel on my bedside table. Now I have nothing to read on the flight.'

It was then that a still, small voice spoke inside me. 'You've a book in your brief-case.' It was my last available copy of a title that I had discovered at the outset of my Christian life, and I had been so impressed with it that, since it was well out of copyright, I had had ten thousand copies printed. It was a nineteenth-century autobiographical account of an English clergyman, the Revd William Haslam, entitled *From Death into Life*. I was intending to give it to a friend in California, and I reminded the Lord of that fact.

'Give it to her.'

'No, Lord, I can't. I've kept it for a friend.'

'Give it to her.' The battle lasted a few minutes, but finally, as the woman pursued her complaint, I said to her, 'I have a book if you would like it.' She thanked me enthusiastically and then saw the title. 'Gee! That's good. I'm into metaphysics.'

She then used the moment to tell her life story. (It was going to be a long flight.) She was the daughter of a clergyman, brought up in a home with a very strict regime. At the age of eleven she had been converted and entered fully into the Christian faith of which she had heard so much. But after a few years it all became too much for her, and she began to look elsewhere for spiritual comfort and insight. She had tried every eastern religion going and various others but had never found satisfaction. When I explained the gist of the book she became very excited. This was interrupted by her husband who growled a rather offensive remark. I decided to tell him of my colleague's tragic death and said, 'Sir, the last time someone said that to me, they died within a couple of days.' There were no further interruptions.

Then the woman said to me, 'I've met you before, you know.' I didn't and said so.

'It was at my home in Northern California.'

'You are mistaken,' I responded.

'Let me explain. I was alone at home and, as I do, I was in meditation. (That did not encourage me as I realized what she was doing had nothing in common with the Psalmist's way of life.) The door opened and you entered the room.'

'I entered the room?' I was incredulous.

'You entered the room, walked over to me, leant over and kissed me.'

'I kissed you?' My voice was reaching an irrational squeak.

'Don't worry, Mister. There was nothing indecent about it. Then you said to me, "I will meet you in my country this fall."'

'I was so convinced of what I had seen that I came to England three months ago in order to meet you. I have travelled throughout the country expecting the moment and ultimately, this morning, as I got on the airplane, I gave up. Then, as I was reading the instructions on the card from the seat, I heard you speak. I didn't need to look up because I recognized your voice – and then I recognized your face after that.

'Mister,' she said, 'you have a word from God for me. What is it?'

A word from God. Little could have been further from my mind. My time had been spent in wrestling with the outrageous fortunes of life to get a seat on an aeroplane, and wondering how I could explain myself if I didn't turn up for a meeting where eight hundred people would be coming. A word from God?

'You think that I have a word from God. Yes, I do. And this is it.' I began telling her of the useless avenues of life through which she had been, but also told her that the commitment she had made to God as a little girl was an unbreakable contract – one that God was still honouring.

When I had finished, she was aglow with God. She replied, 'There's something I must tell you. When I saw you in the vision at my home, you were wearing a regular suit as you are now, except for one thing. Your top coat was a minister's coat just as my father wore, so I recognized it. I think God has called you to express your ministry as a layer of your working life.'

I was stunned.

We never met again. Her husband disappeared into the crowd, still muttering to himself; my last memory of the lady was that she was exultant.

It was certainly a comfort to be aware that my work in the sciences could operate in parallel with anything the Lord had for me by way of Christian work. This was confirmed in some of the meetings in California.

I was approached by a couple who said they would like to pray with me. It didn't occur to me initially that their purpose was to pray for me, rather than for me to pray for them. We prayed and then the lady prayed in tongues. I was surprised and a little embarrassed since, as there were only three of us present and I was the subject of the prayer, it was clear that the husband would have the interpretation of the tongue – and I would be the subject of the interpretation. It did seem rather like a put-up job, but we all waited for whatever God might say.

Then the most unexpected thing occurred: I had a vision. Standing in the open air I found myself looking up into dense, grey clouds which gradually opened so that two small identical objects fell out, tumbling down to the ground in front of me. It was a pair of working boots, designed to reach to the knee – they could have been cowboy boots except that they weren't decorated or leather; they were rubber, more like English Wellington boots, except better shaped to suit my leg. As they hit the ground, instead of falling over they stood upright – waiting, as it were, for me to put them on.

What did it mean? If there was any sense to this, it seemed that God was saying there was a plan for my life that involved my working life as well as some form of ministry that would come down from heaven.

We would find out.

The typical working day can be broken down quite simply into, say, seven to eight hours of sleep, eight hours or so at work, leaving about eight hours to attend to family responsibilities, eating, social life and, if you are a Christian, attending church meetings. For those of us in work, then, our working lives take up the largest portion of our time. So, unless I am to follow our friend from the City of London and leave my Christian faith at the office door, I am struggling with a mismatch in my life. How can I apply my faith in my commercial activities if I cannot find the interaction I seek? Where is the teaching to help me? To what biblical authority can I appeal? On what godly experiences can I rely?

In short, is the church addressing the issues I encounter in my life and preparing me for them?

An international company, for whom I was acting as a consultant, approached me to undertake the design of a gas turbine engine from scratch. The only specification I was given was the amount of power to be generated and the distance required between the engine's main bearings.

This was not a straightforward business and, as I explained, I could not do this alone – it was not the work of one man. To address such a project, I explained, Rolls-Royce used two or maybe three offices filled with aerodynamicists, fluid mechanics specialists, mechanical engineers, performance engineers with computer specialists among them. My hosts then surprised me by saying that there were aware of this and were happy for me to bring together a team to do the job.

I approached friends and others I could trust, and soon we were under way. A limited company was created, and a suite of software programs with it. One of these programs included an entirely new approach in the gas turbine field and involved a substantial investment of time.

As the potential of the operation began to show itself, I was approached with a take-over proposal. It came from an agent I knew, but when I unwrapped his offer I became suspicious of a hidden agenda, though I couldn't really say why. A substantial sum of money was involved – possibly several million pounds – but I would lose the ownership not only of the software but of the company as well. In addition I felt a responsibility to my colleagues who had trusted me with their own professional lives.

What should I do? Of course I prayed about it, but where might I find help? I knew of no one who could bring me the benefit of experience, and I knew of no directions offered from the Bible beyond generalized pointers for life, and it was by no means clear how I should apply these. Even Luke, the scientist of his day, could bring me no direction in a matter involving gas turbine engines!

I think that this highlights one of the sub-standard styles of Christian living which is the enemy of the real thing. Tick-box Christianity wasn't going to cut it. It would not be enough simply to invoke some general principles and squeeze my problem into a recognizable shape so that – hey presto – my answer was clearly laid out before me.

So here was my problem. I had entered a Christian life in which I was assured of a direct, personal relationship with Jesus Christ. I could talk to him and he could talk to me at any time and under any circumstances. And yet I didn't know what to do.

I prayed, and I waited to see what might unfold.

Shortly after this my daughter, Rachel, and her fiancé were on a day-long Christian conference organized by Ellel Ministries. The conference was only a few miles away from our home near Bath, although my colleagues lived in a range of locations across the South, the agent was in Germany, and the potential sponsor was in the Far East.

In the middle of his address, the speaker paused, dropped his voice and said, 'I feel that I have a word from God for someone here.' He then went on to lay out the exact nature of my business proposal, the nature of the finance involved and the pressure there was to sign. He then finished by saying, 'Do not sign this agreement.'

My daughter turned to her fiancé and said, 'That word is for my father. I know it.'

Now this is the sort of God I want to serve. Primarily, I'm not interested in the poetry of what is said, nor in the historical connotations of a word given, but I am interested in a word that is direct, meaningful and comes with an anointing from the Holy Spirit.

Not that I left things there. After Rachel had reported the word to me, I drove into Bath and met the speaker to explore what he had to say about the matter. He astonished me by saying that he was as surprised as anyone to have this word. He was actually quite reluctant to make any claims for its validity. He didn't need to. I knew that God had spoken and I acted upon it. I broke off the discussions with the agent.

That, however, was not the end of the matter. Soon my potential sponsors and the agent were lining up with legal claims against me. A raft of litigation lawyers was flown in from New York to take me to pieces. (I later learned that their fee was about £10,000 each per day. These people represented a very famous – and infamous – company, and they meant business.) In my defence I mentioned that I had an unease with the agent but was unable to pinpoint anything.

That seemed to be enough. The potential sponsor evidently uncovered something, as the agent was summoned to his headquarters. I do not know the detail of what was discussed but I do know that he left the meeting without a job.

Can a place be found for God at the company directors' table? Can he be relied upon to guide his people? Will he conduct matters with justice and mercy? Is he the same in this area of living as in all others?

The answer to all of these questions is an unqualified yes.

What was there for me to learn from these events? Still the most remarkable thing was to be reminded that God speaks to his people. Personally, I have never been comfortable with simply applying general principles from the Bible: apart from anything else, it puts the more creative person at a distinct advantage when compared with someone like me who lacks those imaginative qualities. But to have a relationship with the God who is able to speak to his people in any situation is a different matter. This is the Christianity about which I read in the Bible.

Secondly, there was the fact that, when God speaks, he says something. If I am interested in abstract poetry, then there are volumes to which I can turn – I don't need a prophetic word for that. In fact, I can access innumerable books that will bring me comfort or lift me up. The one thing I cannot do is to find a book on my library shelves that will bring me clear, unambiguous advice or direction – what should I be doing now, what decision should I be making in this complex situation? And it is that dimension that makes us into mighty men or women of God.

This, I discovered, was how the failures of life were to be dispelled and the fears in life brought low.

A new way of life was opening up.

# 9.

# You Must Be Born Again

I had been invited by the BBC to be part of a panel examining the question of why the church is diminishing in size and influence, and I found myself alongside a number of luminaries including a bishop in the Church of England. The TV programme was going out live and the panel's individuals put forward a variety of opinions. Eventually, the presenter solicited my opinion, presumably expecting some scientifically based thoughts. Perhaps the church would be advised to move with the times, introduce aspects of scientific thinking into its agenda, maybe a synthesis of theology with the best that science had to offer. Or maybe I would suggest parallels between the life of the church as we know it and principles of scientific thinking. Perhaps the Second Law of Thermodynamics could bring something weighty enough to satisfy the assembled dignitaries.

If any of this was expected, I must have disappointed. Casting caution aside, I said that the only way in which the church would grow was by declaring the message of salvation, that man must be born again. And I went on to say that, until the church was made up of people who had themselves known the experience of being born again, this would not happen.

The response from the bishop was volcanic. How dare I go about making such outrageous comments? In his churches there were many fine folk – ladies, for the most part – who gave their time and their offerings to further the work of the church and without whom the church would be the poorer . . . in fact, may cease to exist in some rural parishes. These people, the bishop wanted me to know, would make no claim to be born again – in fact, they were not born again – but that did not diminish, in any way, what they did as Christians and that they were, in consequence, Christians.

My reply didn't smooth the waters: we should take note that it was Jesus who said to a religious man, 'Marvel not that I said unto thee, Ye must be born again' (John 3:7). Evidently my status as a layman in his theological world militated against me. While I could be allowed to pronounce on scientific issues that might impinge on the church, there was no way I would be allowed to step over the boundaries into his domain. He was the spiritual man at the table, supported by other spiritual people (off-screen), and their ownership of all things spiritual should not be challenged. It was clear that, if anyone had the authority to quote the Bible, it was him; and, in any case, that was quite unnecessary.

The chairman, sensing trouble, changed the subject and gave me no opportunity to speak again in the programme. In that way, the good name of the BBC was preserved, the programme came to an end and we all went off feeling more or less satisfied.

What is it that creates such strong reactions in people who hear about being born again? Why did Jesus use this term?

The words 'born again' translate from the Greek *gennao* and *anothen*. While the first refers to being born, the second has more than one interpretation – 'again' or 'from above' – which can be useful as a means of expressing the same matter in different ways.

Sometimes that difference is crucial.

Responding to an invitation to undertake a three-week itinerary in Malta, Elizabeth and I landed in Valetta to be told that, after a rest and initial briefing, I was due to speak at a monastery in town that very evening, where a congregation of seventy or so mainly Jesuit priests was waiting for me. I took as my subject the relationship we may have with Jesus Christ. When I had finished speaking, the chairman invited Elizabeth to speak for a while. Afterwards he concluded by saying to his audience, 'Brothers, this is real, and we should note it.' I later learned that this was probably the first time in several hundred years that a woman had spoken in those surroundings!

Later that evening, my host said, 'Tomorrow morning I will be having many telephone calls from all over the island from churches that will want you to speak.' And it is here that he warned me to adapt my language a little. 'Please don't use the words 'born again' because of what they mean in our community. *I* know what you mean, and I know what the Bible says, but to the Catholic clergy on Malta it indicates that a person has abandoned the Catholic Church to join a Protestant one.' He went on to explain that the words were devoid of spiritual meaning and understood entirely in terms of denominational affiliation.

'But what can I do?' I responded. 'Half of my language is taken away at this moment.' Then I recalled how the Greek words of John Chapter 3 could quite correctly be translated as 'born from above' so I offered to use those words. Problem solved. And so there was a successful series of meetings in which I spoke, not on being born again, but on being born from above. Churches, schools, the Catholic radio station and then a major secular station heard about being born from above.

There was one further problem coming. 'I have just had a message from the Archbishop of Gozo (an off-shore island to the north-west in the Maltese group). He has ordered that I get you to Gozo where he will assemble all of his priests and you will tell them what it is to know Jesus. Roy,' my host added, 'in the Catholic Church orders from archbishops are obeyed. We must go.' The next morning we took the ferry from the mainland.

During the crossing, I was further instructed, 'Things are different in Gozo and language means different things here. You can't use 'born from above' in Gozo as that's associated with the trans-substantive beliefs of the bread and wine in the communion service. You are going to have to come up with something different to hit the target.'

Much gazing over the side of the ship at the bow wave curling away finally brought a response from me. 'How about "born anew"?'

'That does it,' I was assured. So the eighty monks who comprised the spiritual core of the island listened and responded to the challenge of the cross, realizing the need to be born anew.

The problem we all have in understanding this conundrum was evident to Nicodemus when he posed his question, 'How can a man be born when he is old? Can he enter his mother's womb and be born again?' Resolving the confusion that Nicodemus had, and which stalks us today, Jesus spoke of two different modes of birth, 'by water and by spirit'. It is this division that separates all the best from the worst that man can experience and clearly points up what derives from the Holy Spirit. This is what defines the Christian life and should characterize the life of the church. We have forgotten this basic division and the result is confusion. The sign of life in the church is not that something is happening: it is that what is happening has the hallmark of the work of the Holy Spirit on it. And that means that Jesus is glorified. Nothing else has any traction.

What Jesus shared with Nicodemus was clearly going to disturb and astonish him, so we should not be too upset if the same message has this effect today. When making a point that we know is going to give our listeners a problem, we naturally prepare them for the unexpected. And so here, knowing all about Nicodemus, Jesus was effectively saying, 'Even taking account of your background, your upbringing, your education – both general and religious – and your experience of life, and further, even your dedication to God's people, there is something I need to say to you, Nicodemus. The fact that it generates such a reaction in you merely emphasizes the imperative of my statement. Nicodemus, you need to enter a new life in me, so new that I can only describe it as being born again. This is not an option, Nicodemus, it is a must.'

And the evidence from subsequent testimony is that Nicodemus did enter in; he became born again.

This incident emphasizes that Christian ministry is at root a one-to-one exercise. I may be standing before a dozen or so at a dinner, a hundred or so in a church meeting, or thousands in a convention hall, but as far as each hearer is concerned I am speaking to one person. So what of all the others present? John Donne wrote in 1624 that 'no man is an island' (*Devotions upon Emergent Occasions*), but in this regard that is exactly what he is. No one can make the commitment for me, and I can make the commitment for no one else. In those moments when I had sat in a church pew, listening to the preacher, it was with horror that I had realized all he was saying was applicable to me. There might as well have been no one else present. This was a heart-to-heart of the most uncomfortable sort. But it did its work and, within minutes, I was born again.

How does it all work? A range of theological positions use different terms and emphases to describe the same event. And so the Calvinist will underline the primacy of God, as the Father draws the soul to Christ (John 6:44); while the Arminian declares that we should seek after God and love him with all our heart if we wish to be saved (Luke 10:25-27). Each is right, even if the expression differs, but the important point common to both is this: there is a coming together and identifiable meeting between God and man.

Now, we all use a language which is at best ambiguous. We say that we meet God when we enter a church building, when we join in a church service, when we pray, and so on. If that is truly so, then there is much to rejoice over . . . but there is a question to be asked. Did each of these events result in a life-changing or at least life-enhancing experience? If not, then we are hardly talking about the kind of meeting where men left their nets to follow Jesus, abandoning work and home and all. That was their call; it may well have a different structure today, and the details will be different, but the call for commitment is no less now than then.

Of course, we are referring to events that took place about two thousand years ago. Could we expect such things today, or has the twenty-first century a more enlightened approach? Maybe we should not expect people to be born again, since their physical, material and spiritual needs are not of the same order. Perhaps today's Christian is more philosophical, better educated, less superstitious . . . more knowledgeable than our predecessors.

We shall see.

One of the earliest events in my learning process was to attend the church's parish weekend at a residential centre where we could enjoy fellowship, prayer, singing and general teaching for the Christian life. There were about forty of us from our church at the centre which, because of its size, accommodated another, similarly sized group from another church. There was no problem in knowing who was from which group – we didn't speak to them and they didn't speak to us! It seemed the dining hall had an invisible line down the middle: our lot turned right to find seats, theirs turned left, and neither infringed the other's territory. Until the crisis occurred, that is.

Arriving a little late for a meal I wandered into the dining hall and, to my dismay, found that all of the seats on 'our' side of the room were occupied, while just one seat remained on 'their' side. I approached it cautiously. At the table sat three amazons, on sentry duty. I asked if I might sit with them. The response was less than enthusiastic but I took the seat and the hitherto animated conversation at the table immediately froze into silence. I felt welcomed!

To break the silence, I opened the conversation with something like 'and isn't it great that Jesus is alive on a day like this?' I was viewed with a mixture of disdain and pity, as one of the ladies responded, 'It depends what you mean by Jesus being alive.' This floored me, so I made a brief reference to the resurrection. Clearly viewing me as a pitiable fellow, one of the team said with tired dismissal, 'You don't believe that, do you?'

'Well, yes, I do.' By way of reinforcing my position, I added, 'The Bible says so.'

'Ah, yes. The Bible . . .' Distant memories were clearly being recalled.

'But no one believes that Jesus rose from the dead . . . not actually rose from the dead. Oh sure, there was a sort of spiritual resurrection, so he is with us in spirit, but as for coming out of the grave, that is quite impossible. People don't rise from the dead. Medical science has shown that that cannot happen.'

Thoughts raced through my mind. If Jesus had not been raised from the dead, who on earth was I talking to when I prayed? And perhaps more importantly, who on earth was talking to me when I prayed?

I needed help and sought it from the pastor. Don Brown was an amiable fellow who never got rattled. He heard me out while sucking on his pipe, then burst out laughing and said, 'Roy! If you want the answer, just read the Bible. Read the Bible.' And with that, he turned away, stuck his pipe further into his mouth and walked off laughing.

One of the first lessons of my Christian life had been learned. Just as I had volumes written by prestigious authors who laid out for me the elements of thermodynamics, fluid mechanics, mathematics and all of the associated sciences, so I had a reference book to hand, my Bible, and the contents would become part of my experience as I practised them.

So I did, and the contents became part of me.

One thing that stays sharp in the memory over the years is the moment a Christian, for the first time, leads someone into this vital relationship with the Lord. For me, the circumstances were unusual. As a new Christian I had spent the evening sat at the back of a tent crusade. In the congregation were one or two people I knew. In particular, there was Chris who came from the same village as I did. With him, there was Tony whom I had never seen before – short, quiet, and carrying a Bible of enormous proportions.

At the end of the meeting I was introduced to Tony. Knowing of Chris's dedication to the Lord, and also impressed with the size of Tony's Bible, my first comment to Tony was, 'And when were you born again, Tony?'

Sourly, he replied, 'I have not been born again.' That almost stopped me in my tracks yet, upon further enquiry, I learned not only that this man was not a Christian, but that he had no Christian origins, had never read any form of Christian book, knew absolutely nothing about the Bible, had never been in a church service in his life before this evening, and had parents who had carefully brought him up in a secular environment. From a spiritual perspective, this man was a blank canvas.

I also learned that he was a Fellow (and possibly the youngest in the university) of Trinity College in Cambridge about fifteen miles away, and it was in the middle of our conversation that that fifteen miles assumed a special importance to us all.

Standing outside the tent and having stated his position as an atheist, Tony swept an arm dramatically across the night sky: 'I cannot believe that there is a thinking mind behind all of this.' It was then that it dawned on Tony that, from the depths of a small town in Huntingdonshire, his bed in Cambridge was about as accessible as those distant constellations . . . he had no means of getting back into town! An offer to drive him back into Cambridge was gratefully accepted, even though he must have realized he would be exposed to further conversation with the maniacs from the backwoods of deepest Huntingdonshire.

We were about half way back to Cambridge when Chris announced, 'Roy – I believe that we should pray.' I wasn't sure whether Tony or I was the more alarmed, but I was able to interject quickly, 'Chris, the Bible orders us to watch and pray; you are the one driving, so you watch and I'll pray.'

We arrived safely and by way of thanks (probably for still being alive) Tony invited us into his rooms for tea. Chris, to whom the inside of a Cambridge College was a mystery, was keen to accept, and so we were led to Tony's staircase.

It was about half-way up this staircase, our footsteps echoing for all to hear, that Chris decided this was the moment to sing some choruses. The whole of the staircase was thus encouraged to 'expect a miracle every day, expect a miracle when you pray; if you expect it, God will show the way; so expect a miracle every day.' Doors on every landing opened as startled, enquiring faces peered out to discover what on earth was going on. I was heartily longing that the earth would swallow me up. It did not, and so all embarrassment in being publicly identified as a Christian, not to mention lunatic, was thus dealt with for all time.

We reached Tony's set of rooms and thankfully closed the door on the world outside as it descended into chaos in our wake. Tea was served in mugs and we sat down as Tony launched his arguments. He began by outlining his primary question, a carefully constructed argument which was quite devastating. Having finished his argument at this point, he asked me how I would answer him. I had no idea. I couldn't actually understand what he was driving at, other than that he was trying to show the impossibility of the Christian case.

There was a pause while we all tried to amass some sort of response, but the silence was broken by Tony adding, 'But I imagine you would say . . .' and in a matter of moments, he demolished his own argument.

I was very anxious to agree with him. But then, pursuing his initial point, he said, 'But that being so, I would then say . . .' Another impossible scenario was laid out, and to this I again had no answer. He responded to himself, however, with the further point, 'And I suppose you would say that . . .' Again, he had a brilliant answer. And so this argument continued, Tony making killer points only to answer himself with brilliant ripostes, until after about six such exchanges, he paused, thought at some depth, then said, 'I'm convinced. You have convinced me.'

I looked at him in blank astonishment, having been no more than an observer in the whole mental battle. Was this what witnessing was all about? If so, I would do more of it.

'So what do I do now?' This man was in earnest. I was confused, but I managed to say, 'You have to repent of your sin.'

'And how do I do that?'

'You pray, and ask the Lord to forgive you for your past life . . . and ask him to become your Lord and Saviour.'

'I'll do that right now.' Tony was clearly not going to miss out on anything and, without hesitation, he astonished me further by throwing himself on his knees. I said to him, 'Tony, you are an educated man. Use your own words to ask the Lord into your life.' And that is what he did. Such was the intensity of the moment that I watched in astonishment as tears began to stain the carpet beneath his bowed head. Of this there was no doubt, there was a paradigm shift in Tony: he had been born again. He wept his way into the kingdom of heaven.

This piece of history was to take an unexpected turn. A couple of months later I was back in Cambridge to do searches for some information for my own thesis. One library, filled with aeronautical material, was well known to me. It was with some surprise, therefore, that I found myself seeking direction from a young librarian I had not met before. She led me down various aisles and through multi-tiered shelves to find the elusive reference. As I dutifully followed I felt a pang of sympathy for her, probably doing many hours of searching in the semi-darkness of the further reaches of the library, possibly never meeting other people. Here was someone who could really benefit from knowing the Lord. So, between the Proceedings of the Royal Aeronautical Society and the American Society of Mechanical Engineers, I asked her if she knew Jesus.

The look of shock on her face told me everything. She was speechless. I took out my pocket New Testament and turned up some passages for her to read. She looked terrified, her back pressed against a large rack of books and eyes open like saucers, her arms reaching out as she evidently contemplated climbing the book racks – backwards. I soon realized that this wasn't the way they do it in the 'How To' books. So we emerged from the secrecy of the book cases, me with my required reference and she with her life – for which she appeared to be very grateful.

That was, I decided, a disaster. She could have easily misunderstood my motive in meeting her between the book racks and I could have been in a police cell already. I couldn't begin to imagine what resistance there might now be to this lady ever receiving the gospel. If all went well, I would never see her again.

But it was not to be.

I made a further visit to the same library a month or so later. I was hardly through the swing-door when I was espied by the same girl. She rushed over to say hello – it seemed she had been waiting to meet me again. Could I tell her more about Jesus, and how he could have a relationship with her, how he could change her life; would he do that and what should she do? I advised her to pray and said that if that presented a difficulty for her, I would pray for her directly.

'When?'

'Right now.'

'Where?'

'Right here.' Except that 'right here' was within view of dozens of students. 'Is there somewhere a little more private where we could pray?' I asked.

'In the stock-room. I have the key. Follow me.'

So, with dozens of eyes boring holes in our backs, and not being sure exactly what we should look guilty about, we decamped to the stock-room. As she bowed her head expectantly we prayed together and she gave her life to the Lord, asking him to deliver her from her past. When she looked up from her prayer her face was full of hope.

I recommended that she pray regularly, read the Bible and get into fellowship with other Christians. But here was my problem. Although there are many Christian contacts in Cambridge I didn't know them: my Christian life had been born in a village fifteen miles away where my subsequent growth had centred. The only Christian I knew in Cambridge was Tony, the Fellow from Trinity College. Half-heartedly, but with no real alternative, I suggested she meet with him.

It was another month before we met again. She was doing well and was now part of a church, involved in the Sunday School teaching programme and fully active in the life of the church. And Tony from Trinity? Yes, she had met him as I had asked – just the once and had seen no more of him. I was pleased, and there the matter rested.

A few months on from this, I was in one of my now less frequent visits to the University when I met her for what turned out to be the last time. All was well, her spiritual life was now well established: she was a mature child of Christ. Her church contacts were secure and work in various societies ongoing. Had there been any contact with Tony at Trinity?

'Well, yes.'

'Really. Should you see him again, please give him my warmest regards, will you?'

'I will. As a matter of fact we're meeting for lunch today.' After a pause in which I grasped the news, she added, 'There is something I'd like to tell you. Tony and I are getting married in three weeks' time.'

Through such experiences as these I was learning the Christian life. Hitherto success in life had been based on intellectual attainment, learning a particular methodology and applying it to advance my position. But this new life was something different: excellence was judged by my walk with God, by hearing his voice and following in humility.

In the matter of who is and who is not a Christian, I have found it necessary not to presume anything. There could hardly have been a better place to learn of this life than Wales, the land of revival.

I was one of four speakers at a conference for 150 Anglican clergymen and my remit was to give one address. One of the four speakers and I were to wind up the proceedings. After reading the passage from which he intended to speak, he suddenly and unaccountably took fright and froze. Try as he might, no words would come out of his mouth and, while the pages of his Bible were turned in ever more frantic gestures, nothing emerged. Finally, in great embarrassment both to himself and his audience, he was gently led back to his seat.

The stage was now empty except for the line of speakers sitting towards the back of the platform. In desperation the conference chairman looked around and, seeing I was next in line, called me out to speak (he really was desperate!). I chose to speak on the Scripture already chosen. I can, with gratitude, report that God honours his word and fifteen of the clerically collared men responded positively and clearly to a call for salvation – including the bishop, a matter of considerable astonishment to me and no doubt to many. Like Tony, and like the librarian from the aeronautical library, they made commitments to the Lord and were born again.

On another occasion in Wales I was speaking one Sunday morning at a church whose denomination, born in revival, was true to the Bible. Towards the end of the service I challenged the congregation in the matter of this vital relationship they might have with Christ. A number responded, among whom was an elderly man. Later on he came and spoke to me quietly: 'I am a minister ordained in this denomination. I have ministered here all of my life, until I retired recently. I have never before heard the message you brought today – so I have never preached it. This morning I realized that for the whole of my life I have missed the real point. So I prayed as you challenged us, and asked the Lord that I might be born again.'

Because of the itinerant nature of the work to which I have been drawn, it is entirely normal to be involved in ministry with people and then never to see them again. So it is always uplifting when I learn about consequences in the longer term.

I was speaking in Aberystwyth. As the meeting finished, I was approached by a lady and her daughter who showed great concern over the lady's non-Christian husband. He was at home, critically ill in bed, and not expected to live. Would I visit him? Of course I would, and so the next day, accompanied by a local Christian man, I went to see him.

We were ushered into his bedroom where he lay, clearly very ill. It was also immediately evident that this meeting was going to be a little different. Here was an angry man – very angry. He was angry about everything, not least because we had invaded his house, his space, his private grief.

Conversation soon became impossible and he drew matters to a close by ordering us out of his house. 'Of course, we will go,' I said, 'but there is just one thing we will do – and you can't really stop us.' As he fumed in bed, we prayed for him very briefly, and then escaped.

And that might have been an end to it, but for the fact that I was speaking at a dinner in a hotel dining-room in Holyhead on the island of Anglesey two days later. I spoke for a while, got rather excited about life and then made a challenge for people to come to the Lord for the new birth.

As I invited them to stand in silence, to my astonishment I saw standing at the table directly in front of me the man whom I had last seen in bed, unable to move. He stood with head bowed alongside numerous others. There was a strong sense that this was a holy moment as we asked God to meet those who were offering their hearts to him now, and I anticipated saying a simple 'Amen' and then sitting down.

But it seemed that the Lord had some other work in mind. The whole assembly stood in silence for what must have been at least five minutes. No one wanted to move. Then we all heard a continuing ringing sound. As it became louder, I opened my eyes to see that the noise was coming from the table in front of me: it was shaking in an increasingly violent way – the crockery, the glasses and the cutlery were all rattling away. It was then I realized that the man who had ordered me out of his house was holding the edge of the table with both hands as he stood, eyes closed, shaking in the presence of God as the Holy Spirit did his work.

It was an astonishing moment. But was there any consequence?

I later received the first of a series of letters from him – progress reports that would stretch over a number of years. He had certainly been born again and wondered what he should do next. The next letter reported that he had led every member of his family to the Lord, so what now? He owned a company with, I think, fifty-two employees. He took the whole company by coach to a Billy Graham Crusade, and he could report that every member of his company was now a Christian. What next? I last heard from him as he was travelling around Africa founding orphanages.

All of that had its genesis at the bedside of an angry man who told us to get out – but not before a brief conversation and a prayer.

Elizabeth and I now live in the countryside a little east of Cirencester in the Cotswolds about eighty miles west of

London. We are within a mile of a village called Harnhill where there is a Christian Conference Centre. Whenever possible I go to the Wednesday evening meetings there, and sometimes I speak. Quite recently I encountered a young lady going from the car park to the meeting. She was aglow and clearly wanted to talk.

'I was here when you last spoke about three weeks ago,' she told me. 'You said that people who didn't know Jesus should give their lives to him at that moment.' I recalled the moment with some embarrassment. It had not been scheduled in any way, nor did I plan to address the subject, when it occurred to me there may be one or two unconverted people there. I made what I considered was one of the weediest gospel challenges I had ever made. Frankly it had seemed like a total waste of time.

'So,' she went on, 'I did what you said, and since that moment I know that something has happened. I don't know what it is, but I feel such complete joy. I'm free from the past, prayer has become meaningful and the Bible has taken on a new meaning for me. What do you think has happened to me?'

'To be honest, everything you're describing is the evidence of new life. You have been born again.'

## 10.

# Understudy to the Great Physician

The earliest days of a Christian life can be a breathless affair – certainly they were for Elizabeth and me. We really had no idea where we were going or what we were doing, and everything that happened represented a new experience.

In a very short while a small group of like-minded people had taken to gathering at our home on a Tuesday evening, where we would read the Bible, discuss matters of interest and pray a lot, all led by David who cared for us like a hen for its chicks, encouraging and teaching all the while. As I have already mentioned, David knew the answers to any question we had – and we had plenty – and, among other things, he taught us to pray over situations that concerned us.

It was at this time that we learned of a twenty-seven-year-old girl living on the other side of the village who had just given birth but, when she tried to sit up after the birth, had collapsed in great pain. The problem was diagnosed: her spine had collapsed like a telescope. It turned out she had a congenital problem, resulting in her spinal column lacking the discs that intersperse the vertebrae. I was told that this problem was unknown in medical science, although I cannot confirm that; certainly it was unusual, to put it mildly.

The prognosis was not good. She was told that she would spend the remainder of her life lying on her back, and she must never attempt to move. This struck us all as intolerable. She would never have the pleasure of playing with her child, never do any of the things a parent would do. She would watch the child grow from the confines of her bed, never to see it running around, much less run with it.

So we all prayed for her. We didn't know her name, had never seen her and, to my knowledge, never have. We were unsure how to pray. Teaching we had received so far did not touch upon healing in any form, and our knowledge of the Bible had still not progressed from John 1:1.

In retrospect I have had to conclude that God is less interested in our smoothly crafted prayers or our carefully polished theological arguments than he is in the condition of our hearts. I'm pretty certain that we prayed the wrong words in the wrong way; we didn't quote the right Scriptures at the right time. In fact, I don't recall that we quoted the Scriptures at all, such was our ignorance.

After a couple of weeks we learned that the doctors had revised their opinion and that she might be lifted just a little. This was a huge encouragement to our dedication to pray. In a further week we learned that she could sit up. Soon after that she began to walk, gently at first, but then reached the point where the specialists told her they could find nothing wrong with her. She was advised to abandon the steel tube that had been made for her body (by a bespoke armour-maker!) and simply to use a firm corset. As far as they were concerned, they didn't need to see her again.

In six weeks, ever since the prognosis had been made and she had faced the prospect of a life lying immobile on her back, this young woman had received the promise of a normal life of parenthood. We were open-mouthed, hugely excited and much encouraged in our Christian walk. Fortunately for us there was no one available to explain that this kind of thing couldn't happen.

And yet not all were healed. Why was that? We do not have all the answers, but it is worth pointing out that the Bible doesn't shrink from mentioning that category of person: at the poolside, for instance, or on the roadside, or at the gate of the Temple (John 5:5; 9:1; Acts 3:2). Of this I am convinced, however: God has a timetable as well as a purpose. He is not in the business of rewarding, in a preferential sense, people who have 'done the right thing'. His is always a work of grace. He will heal people not because of who they are or what they have done, but because of who God is and what he has done.

Now, this is also an encouragement in my own ministry. The fact that a person may not throw away his white stick or Zimmer frame, or jump from his wheelchair or off a stretcher, in the instant he is prayed for, does not spell failure for the praying minister or for the hopeful recipient. Rather it is a prompt to be importunate – to keep on keeping on in the business of prayer.

Furthermore, as I have said, at this point we had absolutely no knowledge of the healing ministry. I still didn't know how much even David knew at that time. All that I could say of him was that he didn't seem to panic, whatever the circumstances. If David really was never more than five minutes ahead of us in Christian experience, then none of us had the seniority in the ranks of prayer warriors to go beyond making the tea!

The disciples who followed Jesus were quite simply instructed to go out and 'heal the sick . . . raise the dead' (Matthew 10:8). I have no record that they did a degree on the subject. Not one held an office or title in his synagogue, as far as we know, and only once in the whole of the biblical record do I know of the instruction that the elders of the church should be sent for (James 5:14). It seems to me that Jesus chooses those who are least qualified, but *prepared*, to respond to his call.

'Whom shall I send, and who will go for us? . . . Here am I. Send me' (Isaiah 6:8).

Of course, healing can and often does come through a trip to the doctor and the medical procedures that may follow. But even here, God is still very much involved, and may at times be pleased to sidestep the 'normal channels' that we have come to expect in Western society.

We have three children (all now big enough and old enough to keep their parents under control). David is our youngest. He had a normal healthy life for three years or so until things began to go wrong. There are two unconnected incidents to mention here.

I was scheduled to speak at some meetings in Llandudno in North Wales. The area was in the grip of severe winter, and heavy snow had closed all the main roads. As the day drew to a close I listened intently to every weather report.

I sat, rather impatiently, in the living room of our home, across the fireplace from Elizabeth as we read our books.

David was on the floor between us, playing with his toy cars. The silence was broken by Elizabeth saying quietly, 'Roy, watch David, will you? He is doing something rather odd.' David was reaching for one of his toy cars but not lifting it. After some moments he looked up and said, 'Mummy, why doesn't my car come into my hand when I try to lift it?'

We looked more closely at David and, for the first time, noticed the condition of his eyes. To our amazement, we saw that they were severely crossed, a misalignment in excess of 25 degrees. Alarmed, we prayed fervently. And then, without denying God's power in any way, we sought medical attention. A specialist chose to do surgery, a fraught business in which we had no idea of the outcome.

I think the anguish surrounding this type of event can only be understood by a parent who has been through the experience. Of course we carried on praying as we took David through the harrowing preparation for surgery. Questions were never far below the surface: our prayers didn't seem to be answered – why? Were we being disobedient to God in allowing the surgery to advance? Would David come through the surgery all right? Statistics for this type of surgery did not encourage us: could he be going irretrievably blind? What would life have in store for him in the event of there being a problem?

David was wheeled off to the operating theatre, a helpless little scrap of a child. Our child.

We prayed and we waited. When he was brought back he was lying down, eyes bandaged. The prognosis was good and the surgeon was positive in his assessment. We were warned not to let David take water since it may induce vomiting with a body full of medication, and the violence of being sick could destroy the good work of sewing his eyes up after the surgery. So, when he woke, what was it that David wanted . . . ? We saw him feel his way along the bedside table to find the water jug, whose contents he demolished very promptly!

In due course, the bandages came off and we saw his eyes for the first time. An elation that he could see was soon tempered by the observation that there was still a misalignment, maybe by about 10 degrees. The surgeon recommended a similar but simpler operation.

In a state of emotional exhaustion Elizabeth and I prayed once more.

'Lord, we can't go through all of this again. We know that you can straighten his eyes without any problem. Please do it for David.'

In order to force his eyes to be straight, David was prescribed spectacles which were worn continuously. This was now at a time when we were feeling challenged over the nature of our commitment to the Lord: should I be offering myself for some form of full-time work for God? Elizabeth felt this challenge most acutely, knowing that in going along this path all of our aspirations as a family would lie in tatters. What of family life? What of a home? What of work to be done? How could we live? What about our parental responsibilities?

It was while she was praying about this that she felt the Lord ask her, 'Would you let me have Roy working for me full-time?' This was not something that she could answer easily. There was nothing romantic about it, or even appealing, least of all to me.

'Lord, if that is what you want,' she said, 'then I will be obedient to you and say yes.' It was then that things began to happen in a most remarkable manner.

Arriving home from school David said to his mum, 'Why is it that I can't see the blackboard properly, Mummy?' Elizabeth encouraged him to sit at school in the front row of his classroom with the best view of the blackboard, but still he could not see.

'You mean that you can't see anything?' Elizabeth asked.

'Oh, no. I don't mean that. Actually if I wear my spectacles like this' – and he perched them on the end of his nose and looked over the top of the lenses – 'I can see everything on the blackboard perfectly.'

Back we went to the surgery, without delay. They were less than enthusiastic. In their opinion a further examination was quite unnecessary since David had been the subject of a detailed examination less than a month previously when the new spectacles had been fitted.

'But we must ask you to take another look at the eyes.' It was under some duress that the surgeon agreed to make a further examination, assuring us that the results would be unchanged.

We watched in silence as he checked David's eyes in every detail. Finally the silence was broken by the surgeon who, looking puzzled, said, 'I have to tell you that there is nothing wrong with David's eyes. They are working perfectly.'

David was, by now, seven years old and the whole matter had lasted for three years. By now we knew pretty well where the health of his eyes was in the scheme of things and we therefore understood why the surgeon was so puzzled.

David had been healed! Of that there was no doubt; the great healer had visited our son.

There is no question that when the Lord does something as monumental as this – restoring a person's sight so that the eyes operate correctly – and that person is your child, the response it evokes is extraordinary. This was confirmation that the Bible doesn't consist of fairy stories or fancy fiction. The book really is a historical record. Looked at the other way round, we can say that the records laid down in the Bible are being repeated in the twenty-first century.

The implications of this are enormous. Maybe I can expect to interact with the God who I discover is not on a cloud over there but has come closer than a brother over here. This is the foundation of the Christian relationship in terms of its outworking and it changes everything. Elsewhere in this memoir I touch upon the operation of the eye in all of its complexity. And as I have gathered these recollections I have been astonished to discover how often we have witnessed the Lord deal with eye problems, whether that is sitting at a hospital bed in England or speaking in a crowded conference centre in Guatemala.

The second incident involving David took place when he was five years old. Shortly after beginning his school life he came home one day with a seriously high temperature. The effect on him was overwhelming and he collapsed. A series of medical examinations led to a prescription of pills but also to the warning that this was a problem he might carry through life: certainly the need for drugs would be ongoing.

This had an entirely deleterious effect on David's life, with what appeared to be a change in his personality, as he ceased to be a bright, interested and interesting child. As Elizabeth and I prayed, we became convinced that we should take David off the medication, trusting in the Lord alone without any medical support.

It should be borne in mind that part of my training as a scientist is to instil a sense of caution. I have learned to question anything that doesn't make sense, however tried and tested it may be. Making decisions for a child's life assumes even greater proportions than when designing an aero-engine. We couldn't be sure of the outcome and a great deal was at stake. What if we made the wrong decision? We couldn't bear thinking about it. We must act by faith.

But faith is not certainty, nor should we ever lead people to believe that it is. To do so would be to risk engaging in some kind of confidence trick, which only results in a greater problem than at the beginning. No; faith carries with it the awful possibility of failure: in fact, without that possibility we are not dealing in the area of faith at all. Maybe we are tempted to rely on precedent. But unless we operate the Christian life by faith, always carrying the possibility of failure, we are in fact in sin, according to the Bible (see Romans 14:23).

For Elizabeth and me, the decision we were making had all the importance of any step of faith we might ever take. If we were wrong in this, the damage to David could well be permanent. Now, this is the word we were convinced that the Lord had for us; in writing this I must stress that it is not intended to be the word for everybody. Not that he doesn't want everyone to be healed, but his detailed plan and timing are special to each individual. Sadly, so-called 'faith' has been invoked in similar circumstances without the personally directed word from God to support it.

With the cessation of his drugs, David's health and demeanour changed remarkably. In an interview with the doctor he spoke approvingly of the improvement in David's condition and then, without asking in any way what regime of medication we were following said, quite simply, 'This is a very good improvement. Keep the medication at exactly the level you are administering it.'

'Certainly we will do that . . .' and we said no more. David's health was restored completely. It was only some time later that I came clean with the doctor, but by then he was not concerned since he had seen David's sickness dispensed with completely.

As I reflected on what had been going on, my scientific rationalism took a pounding. Something was happening that didn't seem to line up with the physics or mechanics that I had learned, or science generally. But I did know this: science throughout its recorded history had been ultimately dependent on observations. While sometimes the observations followed the predictions (as can happen in astronomy), it was the experimental observation that the scientist needed to validate all he held dear to his heart. If I now took the method of scientific observation as the basis for what I was seeing, these events would most naturally point to the direct action of God.

Shortly after these two events in David's life I was invited to be the main speaker at a Christian conference in Indiana on the subject of faith. This was not an entirely happy occasion but Elizabeth and the children were with me and we had good weather. Speaking was a little like treading through treacle, and there was little by way of interchange with the conference delegates.

We had been given a car and driver for the time we were at the conference, and it was the driver with whom I found more contact than with anyone else. 'Tell me,' I asked him, 'do you know what is going on here? Only I realize that I'm not actually getting through to this conference. I can't seem to find any life in it, no response other than just being civil with each other.'

'Of course,' he responded. 'You wear glasses.'

I was stunned. Had I missed something here? Was there a theological nicety that had eluded me over the years?

'This is your problem,' my driver went on. 'The people at this conference believe that to wear spectacles is an admission that you are not healed of your eye problem. So your ministry is automatically useless! If you look, you will see that there is not one person at this conference, other than you, who's wearing spectacles.'

I was not a little surprised but checked my memory of those people I had encountered at the conference. Sure enough, no one else wore spectacles.

'And what of yourself?' I asked. 'You don't need spectacles either?'

Turning from the windscreen of the car, he looked at me and said, 'Well, no, actually. The only way I could be here is not to wear my specs.'

'Do you mean that you do actually have spectacles prescribed?'

'Oh, yes. I'm as blind as a bat without them, but I just keep going.' He then looked ahead again – I'm not certain whether to kid himself or to kid me that all was well.

For me, faith was mustered immediately and in desperation. I recall that, after that, I had a keen desire to walk everywhere.

Did these extraordinary physical healings form any kind of pattern, or was each one an aberration of sorts, a 'one-off' from which we cannot draw conclusions?

This was a question I was bound to ask with every scientifically trained fibre of my being. And over time I reached an answer. Yes, a miracle can happen more than once; and so, being repeated and repeatable, there would be grounds for drawing a conclusion within the domain of scientific enquiry.

Immediately after the healing of the girl with the spinal problem in our village, a child was born with pneumonia. We learned that the chance of survival was just fifty-fifty. We prayed for the baby who, a few days later, was declared by the doctor to be perfectly well.

Now, I could not actually observe the connection between praying for a sick child and the child's subsequent healing, but this is not unknown in science. When Michael Faraday noticed that the reversal of a current in a length of copper wire caused an adjacent compass needle to swing round, the fact that he couldn't understand what he saw simply drove him to discover more. So I could not ignore the fact that there was likely to be a connection between the prayers for these two families and the solution to their medical problems: the statistical sample was too small to draw a definitive conclusion but large enough to encourage further exploration.

Certainly I could make assessments of what we had encountered. It was clear that the mother whose back had been restored, with a set of discs now correctly fitted, was testimony to a violation of the First Law of Thermodynamics. Discs had been created where there had previously been no discs. Pneumonia, an inflammation of the lungs, is not quickly resolved without medication, and I can only conclude that what was reported to us constituted a violation of the normal rate of recovery. In each case, so far as I was able to judge, we had witnessed a miracle.

And just as, in my training, I had always been encouraged to go back to the foundations and their associated documents, so now it was entirely natural in stumbling upon this remarkable aspect of the Christian life to do much the same thing: David, our mentor, was always keen that we did just that. 'Roy, go and see what the Bible says.'

And that is what we did.

# 11.

# He Sent His Word

The year was 1971. We had decided to go to the Festival of Light in central London and, in the event, were part of nearly all of the Christians we could imagine to be in the United Kingdom. Many marched from Hyde Park, though Elizabeth and I decided to go straight to their destination at Trafalgar Square.

We arrived early. Long before the main party had arrived with the speakers and singers, we ran into a number of friends and attached ourselves to various conversational groups at different times. At one point, having felt very privileged to have met a well-known speaker, I turned to go as a woman grabbed my arm to get my attention.

'Are you a famous speaker?' she asked. Anxious not to encourage her in any way, I replied hastily that I was not, and tried to pass her on to someone more suitable.

'No,' she said, 'it's you I want to speak to. It's about my friend here,' she continued, pointing to a large African gentleman standing just behind her. 'You see, he's dying and has only three weeks to live. Will you pray for him?' I had never been in such a situation before, and I was terrified.

'He is worrying about his children. When he dies, he tells me that there'll be no one to care for them. But I say to him, "Look at this great crowd of people here."' She pointed around Trafalgar Square, now almost packed with people. '"They are your family, your brothers and sisters, who are here to care for your children."'

This didn't seem to impress her friend so, with great hesitation, I said to him, 'Do you believe the Bible? You know the Bible makes promises to those who are ill.'

Frantically in my mind I raced over every scriptural passage I had ever read, to check if there was something about healing I could say. Fortunately, quite suddenly, there was. Three verses flashed across my mind. 'The Bible says that by the stripes of Jesus we are healed. It says that we shall lay hands on the sick and they shall recover. It also says that Jesus healed all those who came to him.' How these had popped into my mind I couldn't say, but evidently they touched a nerve in this man. His face had been creased in pain, but now with a quizzical look he slowly lifted his right hand, clenched as a fist, until it was at the level of his chest and then, with a resounding thump he hit his chest and gasped out, 'The pain. The pain.' Then, after a slight pause he added, 'The pain – it's actually going.'

I looked at him in blank astonishment as he went on to give me a potted version of his life story. He told me how he had followed the Lord for many years but confessed that things had gone wrong. Then he had contracted cancer. 'It was God's punishment in me for my sin,' he said.

'No, that is not God's punishment,' I said. 'He doesn't do things like that. The fact that you have had cancer is not a punishment; but I do believe that God can take the cancer away.'

'But the pain,' he shouted, 'the pain has gone totally.' The joy on his face was beyond description. He lunged forward, embraced me and hugged me. Both his arms had gathered up all of my body such that my arms were trapped by his and my feet were off the ground.

Elizabeth had got separated from me in the crowd and was talking to some people we both knew. They asked where I was. 'He's over there,' she said, pointing in my general direction. She then received a shock as she saw me, feet off the ground, struggling to breathe while trapped in this man's embrace.

As we left shortly afterwards, I tried to explain but words failed me. So I pointed back in his general direction and, at that very moment, I saw something quite extraordinary occur. Along the line I was pointing, about half of the quite tightly packed crowd stepped forward as one, while the other half stepped back. At the end of this suddenly formed human corridor stood the man. His face was lifted up to heaven, and his arms raised as high as he could manage, as he worshipped the God who had met him and healed him.

We arrived home with many memories but none with greater impact than this one. I was mystified by what had happened. It was clear to me that the Lord had healed the man, although I had no medical evidence to support that. But how had the healing occurred?

I had heard that the prayer of faith healed the sick, but I hadn't prayed. I knew that we should lay hands on the sick and they will recover, but I hadn't laid hands on the man. I knew that the elders of the church should pray, but I didn't know of any elders around at the time (at that time I didn't even know what an elder was!) So now, in prayer, I asked the Lord to show me what had been going on.

My reading that morning was in Psalm 107 and included verse 20 which put it unambiguously: 'He sent his word, and healed them'. That started a whole new train of thought – that God could heal not just by the standard church-approved methods but by something as simple as speaking the word. Essentially he was going beyond the influence of man, the control and the personal points gained, the prestige and the power that results, to send his word directly into a situation. To speak the word cuts through all the paraphernalia with which we so often clothe the healing ministry and leaves something far simpler in its stead.

We had seen God's word at work. The unscheduled, unplanned yet co-ordinated movement of the crowd of people seemed pretty miraculous to me, but it was evident that what had happened in the man's life was the real miracle. I didn't need the two laws of thermodynamics to prove it to me: it was right before my eyes and I could not ignore what was

This was to lead to the question of what ministry really is and how I could become an able minister of the New Testament, as previously related.

Meanwhile God continued to heal.

If we discount the brain for a moment, then I am told that the two most complex organs in the human body are the ear and the eye. The first occasion on which I saw an eye receive a touch from God was in Central America when I was speaking in Guatemala City during a preaching tour. I had flown to Los Angeles to meet Dr Ernest Soady who lived there and travelled extensively in the Central American region, as well as my friend, Bill Kemp, from the United Kingdom. Our itinerary used airlines that had been set up by Mickey Mouse, so it was entirely normal for arrangements to go wrong. On landing in Guatemala we were given landing cards for another country and this held up matters in the Arrivals hall, as all the details of over a hundred passengers were re-written on the official documents of Guatemala. But this was also to be the location of a remarkable event.

The geography of Guatemala City airport was such that, on landing, passengers walked along a short tunnel at first floor level into Arrivals. Then we made our way down to Immigration on the ground floor via a flight of stairs. Being the last off the aircraft, we could see all the other passengers ahead of us, waiting for Passport Control to check their passports.

Suddenly it was as if everyone stood quite still and then turned their heads to look up the flight of stairs towards me. The sight was astonishing because every person I saw had some serious eye condition: some were blind, others had misalignments, yet more had infections with puss oozing out. The eye conditions were, without question, all serious. I looked in astonishment and then, in an instant, everyone had turned back to continue with the passport business.

What had I seen? The people were real, but the sight of the turned heads and the eyes was a vision – at a time when I least expected anything of a spiritual nature to occur. I had no idea what God was doing, but I knew that something was afoot.

Nor did I have any idea what the Lord's intentions for my life were at this time. I wasn't looking for change: what I had seen and learned by then was quite enough for one lifetime. I had plenty to dwell on in my memory and I had reached a comfort zone in which I felt I could handle whatever life cared to bring.

Our eventual destination was Tegucigalpa, the capital city of Honduras, an area well filled with wars of one sort or another. In the mountain region about twenty miles out there is a fertile valley known as the Vallée des Angeles, the Valley of Angels, and this is where we were headed, to an orphanage with up to 160 children and a wonderful history.

The contrast between the Valley and the City of Angels, Los Angeles, was marked – here things were primitive! As we sat rather disconsolately at the kitchen table of the house we were assigned in the walled enclosure, the Casa Blanca, I chatted with my travelling companion, Bill Kemp. Other than having a coffee grinder on it, the table was bare. As we talked I picked up the coffee grinder. Horror of horrors, from beneath the grinder and through the air cooling duct to the electric motor cascaded dozens of ants. But these weren't just any old ants, they were ants on steroids! The average size was an inch or so. They moved quickly. So did we.

Eventually peace was restored, and Bill and I found some bedrooms in what turned out to be quite a spacious building. We chose our rooms and retired for the night. As I entered the bathroom to clean my teeth, I discovered that the ants were as nothing compared with the rest of the wildlife; for there, immediately above the lavatory on the wall, a scorpion was quietly dozing. I watched him closely (hoping that he wasn't returning the compliment), decided that there was at least a chance that I could move faster than a sleeping scorpion and so, happily recalling how to sweep a ball in my cricketing days, I made the fastest swipe of my hand ever and the scorpion went straight into the lavatory. I pulled the flush to launch the first scuba-diving scorpion in Central America. For my part, I went to bed, not in triumph but simply grateful that in this war with nature I was slightly in the lead.

Bed, though, was a different challenge. There was a single and very thin blanket laid over the mattress that was supported by a steel-tube bed-frame. It was a folding bed and had been created by a maddened sadist who had designed the main folding mechanism to be a bar stretching across the bed about half way down its length. It was a perfect fit for the small of my back: lying on the bed was a quite excruciating event.

I lay in bed plotting my escape. The airport at Tegucigalpa was just over twenty miles away. I wasn't certain how I could book a flight to Heathrow. Everything I thought of involved an impossibility somewhere down the line. I was frustrated, in a lot of discomfort, cold and tired.

Then, in the silence of the night, something of such moment occurred that it is unforgettable. Before my eyes there appeared a picture. I was looking along the muscular forearm of someone, a man with hair from elbow to wrist. He held in his hand a rope which, hanging in the shape of a catenary, stretched out from his arm for twenty feet or so and was tied to a rope halter on a young horse. The grass was trampled flat, and I could see that the horse had walked around its keeper for many circuits, creating a flat, circular path in the grass. Only the horse's head, complete with halter, could be seen. Realizing that the Lord was saying something, I said, 'I don't understand what I am seeing, Lord.'

The picture faded, to be replaced by another – and again, a horse featured centrally. I was now looking not at a young horse eager to rush off and enjoy itself, but at a mature and fully grown Shire horse. It was dark brown, almost black in colour, with a white flash running across the head and between the eyes, another flash on its large, expansive chest and more on its front hooves. It was beautifully groomed, shining in the sunlight, standing in dignified manner above all else about it.

Again, 'Lord, I don't understand what I am seeing.'

He replied, 'In the first picture you are looking at a young horse, full of energy and confidence but it has not yet been broken in. I cannot use it. You are that young horse and I can only use you when you have been broken in – when you learn to hear your Master and, without question, do as you are told. You need to be broken in.'

'And what is the other horse?'

'That is a horse which has been broken in and is prepared to go into the show ring before many thousands of people. It will do exactly as I order it and without question. You see, I know this horse and I can trust it.'

But could he trust me?

The schedule for one week in the Central American itinerary included five talks, one every evening from Monday to Friday in Guatemala City on our way to Honduras. There were about fifteen hundred people at every night's meeting, at which I spoke through an interpreter. As I concluded on the fifth evening, to my surprise the vision I had had at the airport returned – a room packed with people who had serious eye conditions.

I concluded that there were people in that congregation, maybe half a dozen or so, whom the Lord was going to heal of serious eye problems. Turning to the interpreter, I asked her not to dismiss the meeting but to say that the Lord was going to heal several people of serious eye conditions, so if someone in the audience had a condition not treatable by spectacles, they should step forward at that moment.

Over one hundred people came forward, all with terrible eye problems. There before me was the picture I had seen at the airport! I had no idea what to do. To make my position even less secure, my interpreter took fright and fled. My Spanish being non-existent, I had no means of speaking to these people.

I prayed. The people couldn't understand what I was saying, while I couldn't understand what I was doing! I cried aloud to God, asking him to intervene in the chaos I had masterminded. Pointing to one man in the crowd, about half way back in the scrum, I asked the Lord to heal him. To my utter astonishment the man, who I am sure had not noticed me and could not in any case understand what I was saying, suddenly threw his hands in the air and began rejoicing as he realized that God had touched him. So far as I could establish, his eyes had been healed.

Pointing at another person I again prayed from several yards off. The result was the same.

So the evening progressed. I have no idea how many of this large crowd met the Lord at their point of need, but clearly many did. Eventually just two were left standing, a young boy of maybe eleven years and his mother, both distraught. The problem was evidently with the boy whose left eye I could see as he stood about six yards away. It was unbelievably swollen. I concluded that he probably had a tumour behind the eye which protruded from the head so much that the eyelid would not close. The eye itself was a sickly amber colour and turned in towards the nose, such that the boy was severely cross-eyed.

Walking towards him, I began to weep. My son David was just this age, and it was at this time that we were struggling with the major problems in his eyes. So I knew the anguish of this family and wept with them. We prayed, I hugged the lad and returned to a seat in the body of the hall, a little way down one of the two major aisles. As the meeting finished people began to move around, but I stayed in prayer for some moments before standing up. People were filing past and I was just in time to see the lad and his mum returning from the front of the meeting. I looked closely at him.

I could immediately see that the eye no longer stood out from the head. The discolouration had disappeared and so far as I could see the two eyes were now correctly aligned.

It is inevitable that detractors will doubt what has been written here, convinced that such things are impossible and such reports either mistaken or fraudulent. And of course the full array of medical measuring equipment is not always to hand, so the sorts of checks that I, as a scientist, would like to present as definitive proof cannot be offered. In fact, if there was always the required instrumentation to hand, things would be suspicious and suggest a put-up job. Seeing the records of Jesus' ministry, I notice that none of the chroniclers referred to any instruments they had to hand. But that did not discount, in any way, the testimony of the Gospel writers. They recorded eye witness testimony and their records served to change the world.

In the matter of eye problems, however, I can make one report where there is a full medical record.

In England the Cotswolds (the range of hills where I live) are crossed by a major highway that intersects with the M4 motorway to London. Our daughter, Rachel, and her son, Edward, were travelling with us to visit our son, David. I was driving a newly acquired car whose performance impressed me. The weather, however, was less impressive: it was grey and damp.

As we reached the M4 intersection I noticed that visibility was not good so I did a screen-wash. Nothing improved so, concluding that the muck was on the inside of the windscreen, I rubbed it as best I could. Again, no improvement. By now we were on the M4, climbing the long, gradual hill eastbound towards London. After about two miles we crested a rise where an expansive Wiltshire sky opened up before us.

As I looked at this familiar scene, I noticed something very odd. Over the whole of my area of vision, from top to bottom and left to right, were hundreds of tiny black dots. This curious sight continued all the way into London.

When we reached David we sat down for tea, and as we talked I tried a little experiment by closing one eye and looking through the other. Surreptitiously I put my hand over my right eye so that I could look through the left. Other than an annulus of light, I could see nothing. Nothing! I tried again, but there was no doubt. My eye registered a uniform greyness and a thin ring of light which quickly disappeared. Then there was nothing. I had gone blind in my left eye.

When it came time to leave I had still not mentioned anything. In a totally uncharacteristic manner Rachel asked, 'Can I drive the new car, Daddy?'

I readily complied.

I wasn't sure who to discuss this with, but in my office on the Monday morning the telephone rang and it was my good friend, Barry, who was an optician. I told him what had happened.

'Roy,' he responded. 'Forget why I rang. I want you to do something for me. Put the phone down and within the next hour one of my directors will call you to arrange an inspection of your eyes. Go immediately at the time he suggests. Do not delay. I cannot say what is happening, but it's clearly pretty serious.'

I was soon in the office of a Dr Clayton who inspected both eyes very closely. His prognosis was not good. He explained that he could not see a great deal in the left eye since it was full of debris, but he was able to say that something appeared to have gone wrong at the back of the eye. He was going to get me into the Eye Hospital immediately.

By the time we left the Consulting Room, the secretary had already made the arrangements and we were on our way to the hospital where, I understand, lunch was abandoned to deal with me. I was seen by a Burmese specialist. She took almost an hour to examine each eye and then, with authority, gave her diagnosis. She told me that my right eye was in excellent condition but there was a problem with the left eye. I learned that I had a posterior viscous detachment which she explained was a tearing of the rear fixing of the eye from the back of the socket. The tearing had resulted in much debris in the eye which was now the cause for concern. If any of the debris impacted on the retina or the macula, permanent blindness could result. I should wait for three weeks to see if the debris settled, when the specialist could see these components of the eye, and then we would know if there was permanent damage.

I left the hospital in something of a daze. I had to break the news to Elizabeth that I had lost the sight of one eye. Elizabeth, pragmatic as ever, said to Rachel who was there at the time, 'Well, if Dad is going blind I shall have to learn to drive.' Rachel was unsure which would be the greater disaster.

A couple of weeks later I was scheduled to speak one evening at an Anglican church in Pucklechurch just outside of Bristol. I was horrified to discover that the subject fixed for the evening was that of physical healing. With one eye only I was driving rather carefully and so I arrived at my destination only just in time – and with no time to share my problem with the pastor or discuss whether I might actually be disqualified from speaking.

The service got under way and soon I was standing to speak. My audience was attentive, unaware of my problem and unaware of the dialogue going on inside me. The first voice I heard, behind all that I was saying, said, 'You are preaching on healing, but you are not healed yourself.'

My own voice replied, 'That's what I'm here for – to talk about healing.'

'But you are not being honest. You're a fraud. You're talking about being healed but you're not healed yourself. Tell them you're blind in one eye.'

'I can't do that. I'm here to encourage them.'

'But be honest with them. You are blind and you know it. Tell them you are blind.'

'Listen, Satan. This Bible in my hand is the word of God. I am here to preach the word of God. Whether blind in one eye, or even in two, this is still the word of God and this is what I will preach.'

I finished my address and sat down at the front of the congregation. Looking to the east end of the building I realized something looked different from earlier on in the service. The final hymn was well under way and so, with nobody noticing, I lifted my hand, covered my right eye . . . and found that I could see through the left eye.

I could hardly grasp it. An hour before, I could see through one eye only: I had preached on healing, declaring that God was able and believing that the word of God could be relied upon in the face of my own predicament. I hadn't prayed, hadn't got others to pray for me, hadn't actually expected anything in my own situation, but now, over a period of several minutes, my eyesight had returned.

The facts were incontrovertible, but there was more to come. While the eyesight was restored, the tiny black dots remained.

The following Sunday I was sitting in the congregation of a church in Oxfordshire. A flyer on the pews announced that the evening service would be on the subject of physical healing. I asked the curate who was due to be preaching if he believed that God actually healed people. He affirmed that he did, so I pressed on: 'Does God heal today or did he do it only in Bible days?' His answer was cautious but positive so I said, 'Good. I shall be there this evening.' I explained how my vision had been restored but that the hundreds of black dots persisted, and then I concluded by saying, 'I will believe the Lord to complete his work this evening.'

About fifty people had congregated for the evening service and, at the appropriate moment, those who wanted prayer were invited to raise their hands. Naturally I was among them. The curate, along with the lady who had led the service, then moved down the rows of people, praying for the raised hands. When they reached me, I outlined the specific need for prayer and they prayed for me at some length.

'Now, open your eyes and tell me what you can see,' the curate commanded. Good, I thought, that's what I would do if I were the one praying for someone (none of the 'sweet by and by' here). I opened my eyes, looked up and found that all but about a dozen of the little black dots had disappeared.

The residue disappeared over the next two days. Just a few days after that I had to revisit the Eye Hospital. On this occasion, I was seen by an amiable Bangladeshi specialist supported by a quiet English lady. As he struggled to make sense of the notes written by the Burmese specialist I told him what she had diagnosed. After a careful examination of both eyes, he announced with some incredulity that there was nothing wrong with either eye. He wondered why, so I told him about the prayer and what had happened through that time.

He listened attentively and then replied quietly, 'Yes, yes. But you must understand that you are blind. You cannot see.'

'But you have just told me that both of my eyes are in perfect condition.'

'Let me tell you what is wrong,' he said, producing a very large chart which pictured the cross-section of an eye. 'You have much debris in the viscous, but especially it is gathered around the macula, here.' He identified the precise region where all the debris was supposed to be. 'And that is why you are blind.'

'But I am not blind. Look, I can put my hand over my right eye and now I can still see you perfectly using my left eye.'

'But I say that you cannot possibly see. You are blind,' he insisted.

'Why, sir, can I see you then?'

Suddenly, to everyone's amazement, the quiet assistant jumped up, threw her hands in the air and shouted, 'It's a miracle, it's a miracle! Praise God, he's done a miracle for us!'

Thoroughly disorientated and lost for words, the specialist discharged me, asking his assistant to escort me out. As the door closed behind us, the assistant threw her hands in the air again. 'I've worked in this hospital for many years, and every day before I come to work I ask God to show me a miracle. And now he has done it – and to one of my patients! Praise God, praise God . . . I'm going to tell my church about this.'

A subsequent visit to my optician confirmed the specialist's observation, and I have obtained a report from the optician which is reproduced here with permission.

Professor Peacock presented for an eye examination on 3rd July 2007, noting the appearance of what looked like a hair in his vision along with a large number of small floaters and reduced vision in the LE. The 'hair' had been present approximately one week, prior to the eye examination appointment. Examination confirmed a reduction of vision in the L.E. (R:6/9-L6/18)

Further examination inside the LE revealed a significant amount of haemorrhaging from a burst blood vessel in the infero-temporal mid-periphery of the fundus as well as a mass of floaters over the macular area.

It was clear the fundus had been damaged and urgent medical investigation was required.

Professor Peacock was referred immediately to the local eye dept.

On 18th August 2007 I re-examined Professor Peacock's eyes.

Using the same pair of spectacles he had used on the previous appointment, I recorded visual acuity to R:6/6 and L:6/6.

On examining inside the LE I was surprised to find no sign of haemorrhaging or the mass of floaters which had occluded the macula.

Did I, as a scientist, need further proof of the healing power of God in a physical situation? I did not. I was not the subject of auto-suggestion, the medical reports giving clear evidence of what was happening. But in the light of my professional training, should I not be looking at cause and effect in terms that fitted with the philosophy that underpinned my daily work?

Pointless, quite pointless.

This was my eye that had been blinded, it was my experience – I couldn't fool myself and I could now see again. And I didn't want to fool myself, anyway.

There was only one conclusion: the Lord had healed me.

The incident with my eyes provided all of the elements I could hope for in providing for me a testimony with all the confirmations that my scientifically inclined and somewhat cynical nature might demand.

First, there was the immediacy of the story: this wasn't about someone of whom I had never met, or someone I'd met far away or long ago beyond cross-examination.

Second, there was the examination and reporting from several layers of specialist, all agreeing at every detail.

Third, there was the response of a succession of audiences in several meetings at which I spoke.

All in all, I could say that my testimony was consistent, of high quality and gave all the glory to God. So could there ever be a problem with it? Might it still be a source of controversy? As I was to discover, the answer was sadly and most definitely yes.

After one public meeting a young man said he needed to discuss several matters with me. I could see this would take some time and, seeing there was a queue of people to talk and pray, I suggested he wrote to me. His letter was quite astonishing.

Beginning with a brief outline of his scientific credentials and his professional achievements as an optician, indicating that he was the renaissance man equally at home in the field of artistic appreciation and progressive scientific endeavour, he then took some trouble to rubbish the whole story. While, as he explained, God is *able* to perform miracles, he actually doesn't (for reasons I was unable to grasp). He pointed out that all the people who examined my eyes were clearly not qualified and actually at the point of incompetence; the equipment they used had to be out of date (even though the hospital I had attended was the newest in the country) – whereas in his High Street practice he had available the most advanced equipment on offer. He explained the processes in the eye (which I had taken the precaution to read up before going public with my story) and then said that what I reported could happen, but only over an extended length of time. In short, my story was flawed and, by implication, I was a fraud.

While I tried to respond in a simple factual manner, I felt I had to point out that I was there – he wasn't.

Why do people react in such a manner? Why so unreasonable in their reasonableness; so aggressive while, of course, acting in love; implacable yet claiming that the new life has brought freedom? Could it be that exposure to this kind of Christian life carries a threat to the very foundations of their faith – a faith that has not yet been secured or anchored in the reality of God's revelation? Was it all perhaps no more than a dictum learned from the pages of a book, albeit a very fine book? Might it be head knowledge and not something gained from the searching of the heart?

Still, praying for an individual does not always produce the text-book result we anticipate.

Like most areas of the nation to which I have been, I was advised not to bother with going to South Wales. I was told it was 'the evangelist's graveyard', and anyway, I had the wrong accent. Strangely, they had said the same things about the North-East and East Anglia. All very encouraging!

But I went. The occasion was a dinner in the Dragon Hotel in central Swansea, where I had spoken at a conference about a year before. I spoke at the end of the dinner, when a number of people came forward for prayer. I approached one lady, held her hands and said, 'What do you want prayer for, my dear?'

'I have these terrible head pains. They are with me continuously, from the moment I wake in the morning until I go to sleep at night.'

'That's terrible,' I sympathized. 'Tell me, how long have you had these awful pains?'

'Ever since you were here last time.'

# 12.

# When You Pray

It was the driest summer on record, and we were attending a camp at Lee Abbey, an Anglican conference centre in north Devon in the South West of England. There were 140 young people present, and our inclusion was unexpected. It happened that the camp organizers lived a short distance from us in Bedfordshire. They had turned up at one of the Thursday evening meetings where the husband, Ray, had been healed through having a short leg grow. When his physician declared that Ray's leg did not now match the measurement on his record, they had the assurance of the Lord's reality. A relationship ensued, leading to the invitation to join the team at the Lee Abbey camp. I was asked to be one of the evening speakers. I relished the prospect.

On one evening, as I was speaking, a note was handed to me, to be read out immediately. A forest fire had taken hold to the west and south of us and, with the prevailing wind, was expected to engulf the camp by two o'clock in the morning. I asked my audience if they wanted their night disturbed . . . or did they believe that God could put the fire out? With their eyes closed I asked people to pray and indicate if they had faith that God would answer our prayer then and there. When 139 hands went up, we prayed.

One of the team members, a regular at the camps, later reported that he and his wife were outside the marquee and up the hill some way, watching the sky turn red as the flames reached across the hill towards the camp. 'Suddenly,' he said, 'it was as if a giant fire extinguisher had been turned on. Within fifteen minutes the raging fire had subsided, the flames had disappeared, the sky was no longer red and there was nothing on the ground indicating a fire.'

Things happen when we pray.

In the type of work I did in my laboratory it was not unusual to find that the instruments we wanted to use had yet to be invented or developed. This was the case when we wanted to measure the unsteady response of rotating blades in a time-dependent environment. And this too became a matter for urgent prayer.

We needed a class of miniaturized pressure sensors that could withstand the centrifugal force field in a rotating assembly while maintaining sensitivity, enabling them to record the slight perturbations in the flow. So we set about developing such an instrument, complete with a radio transmitter and mounted on the assembly adjacent to the pressure sensor. This involved moving into new terrain and all that goes with the unknown.

It was not a quick job. At first we mounted the instrument on the assembly while it was stationary. The electronics worked satisfactorily. Then the assembly was rotated at various speeds up to the maximum and, again, the checks indicated successful operation. Finally the airflow around the assembly was started and everything set to work. The results confirmed that we had a working instrumentation assembly and we saw, we think for the first time in history, high frequency readings from a rotating assembly operating in an unsteady flow.

Frankly, you have to have done it yourself to realize the sense of elation and excitement at witnessing such an event as this. Doing scientific research involves a lot of sweat and tears and very few moments of unmitigated, jaw-dropping thrill. These are our 'punch the air and jump' moments.

Some years later, while reading some early papers in my current field of interest, I stumbled across a paper by two engineers in which, with no instruments and hence no measurements, they had deduced the transient shape of the waves we were trying to measure. I compared my experimental results with what they said should be happening based only on some fundamental principles of fluid mechanics. And the two sets of data were virtually co-incident. Those men were thinking this through in 1935: I was producing my results nearly fifty years later!

Still, we were now prepared for our programme of research which would engage us for many months. But that was the moment when things went wrong.

One of my team had found a problem. While going through the initial test programme, the signals recorded on a bank of cathode ray oscillographs went crazy. Nothing my colleague could do would eliminate this electrical 'noise'. Along with other team members I watched the rogue readings flitting across the oscillographs. A frequency analysis on an attendant computer, suitably programmed, produced nothing we could recognize, so I left the matter in the hands of the research officers, saying airily over my shoulder, 'Just sort it out.'

An hour or so later the activity around the research rig was intensifying, but still no solution had been found. Realizing this was a potential killer in our work, I transferred as many of the team as I could to work on solving the problem.

One day of investigation became two until, with alarm, I could see the laboratory programmes slipping. By now I was desperate and open to any suggestion from whatever source. Returning to my office, I realized that there was something I had not done: I had not prayed about it. So, standing there in my office, I prayed – as so often – in desperation.

I returned to the rig in the laboratory where all of the team were still investigating. We stood in a disconsolate circle wondering what the next step might be.

'Can I mention something?' Jim's voice was very rarely heard. He was not one of the high flyers in the team. He wasn't a technician, an engineer, a physicist; in fact he was little more than the floor sweeper whose job it was to keep the place tidy. 'I've got an idea,' he continued. Grasping for anything, I asked what he wanted to say.

'I'd like to try something,' he continued. 'Could I try it after lunch, though, as I go home for lunch?' Was he mad? It certainly seemed so, especially to those who saw him come cycling back from home with a brown paper parcel under one arm.

Jim entered the laboratory as everyone watched him in silence. He was clearly rather pleased that, for once in his life, he was the centre of attention. He place the parcel on a table close to the oscillographs that were busy in their game of producing what seemed to be random noise. He then proceeded to unpack a battery-operated radio, and we all watched while he switched on and tuned in. Finally he located Radio One which was playing some indescribable music.

We watched with incredulity as the traces on the oscillographs faithfully followed the modulations of the music in every detail. The problem was immediately identified. Somewhere in our system was a tuned aerial, picking up the radio signal in our frequency. That could only mean that there was an unshrouded lead. Frantic dismantling highlighted the offending wire in a few minutes, and a light cover of lead wound around it soon eliminated the random signals on our equipment. Problem solved.

Now, the question may be asked, 'Could we have solved the problem anyway in due course, or was this really God's intervention in our work?' There is little doubt that the problem would have been solved eventually just by using good engineering practice, but there is more to it than that. The important thing to note is that the problem defied our solution over numerous hours of intensive work, yet almost immediately after I had asked the Lord to intervene the mystifying noise was identified and the problem solved. The cynic would say that this was a coincidence. Archbishop Temple, when challenged in such a matter, had this reply: 'You may well be right, but I find that if I don't pray, the co-incidences don't happen.'

On another occasion I had learned that the British Government had offered help to a nation in the Far East in solving an apparently intractable problem connected to their aerospace industry. This country had a generous budget to pursue research programmes but, for all the money spent on the programme, there appeared to be very little by way of results. My job was to look over the whole of their aerospace research and development sector and offer ways to improve their operation. This involved visiting all of the facilities distributed around the country.

It was a very pleasant job to be doing, travelling across a continent with the sort of perks that are not usually on offer in the scientific business – including my own chef, my own chauffeured car over part of the country. This was not my normal lifestyle! To make life even more pleasant, the problems to which I was introduced all seemed to have a solution that pleased my hosts. That was until I reached the nation's research headquarters.

I was taken to a shining new facility. At the doorway, the foundation stone was pointed out to me, laid eleven years previously by a very famous hand, and then my hosts gave me a tour. This comprised a series of research rigs, each attached to a very large air supply, the air being delivered through a pair of air compressors set in parallel. It all looked impressive but, as we retreated to the air-conditioned control room, my guide was joined by another man who, it emerged, was the Director of the Institute. As we talked, he turned to his colleague, the number two in the Institute, and asked, 'Have you mentioned the problem to our guest?'

'Oh, no sir,' was the reply.

'Why not?'

'Because we are under your orders to tell no one about the difficulty.'

'Why do you think we have invited him?'

'I don't know, sir.'

'To see if he can solve the problem. So, tell him.'

'Tell him?'

'Yes, tell him.'

Number 2 turned towards me and said, 'I need to tell you: we have a problem.'

It was time for me to look surprised. 'Really?'

'Yes. It's this. There are two compressors on this circuit, as you see, but we can't get them both to work together. We've tried everything, even dismantling the compressors from their ductwork, and then each one does work in isolation. But they won't work together. Why is this?'

Frankly, I had no idea, but I felt I should at least try to look competent and in control. 'I would like a full set of engineering drawings of the facility, then I will comment.'

The Director ordered it so, and the command was fed down various levels of hierarchy until someone suitably junior ran from the control room. He returned after some minutes with a roll of paper about six feet long and a foot in diameter. This was laid out on a table, and so I examined a drawing of the main supply duct and the compressors.

I was lost. It had been possibly ten years since I had last looked in frustration at an engineering drawing. I might as well have been looking at a map of the London Underground. What could I do?

I prayed.

For most of my life I have been short-sighted, and anything beyond six feet in distance melts into a soft, out-of-focus picture. Therefore I wear spectacles from morning to night. As I looked at the eight- by six-feet drawing before me, typically out of focus even through spectacles, something quite amazing happened. A circular section in my line of view, about three-and-a-half inches in diameter, suddenly came sharply into focus, the remainder remaining fuzzy. This portion showed the split of the ducting leading into the two parallel compressors. I looked on in total astonishment, the bifurcation remaining at the centre of my attention. The roomful of scientists, engineers and others waited in a somewhat intimidating silence, full of anticipation. Clearly they had more faith than I did!

Looking at the part of the drawing in focus, I reached my hand forward and pointed it out. As one, everybody leant forward. I heard myself say, 'Gentlemen, there is your problem.'

'And the problem is . . . ?'

'At that bifurcation there. You have a fluidic switch.' It occurred to me that I had no idea what a fluidic switch really was.

'What is a fluidic switch?' I was asked.

'I'm glad you asked that,' I replied. I needed to play for time. 'Ah, would you give me a little while to think this through? We're at the end of the day, so maybe we could convene again tomorrow morning when I will give you my thoughts.'

I was driven to my hotel, the Ritz. What was a fluidic switch? I recalled that I had had a student working for me some years before. He had become enthusiastic about a new sector of science known as fluidics and, without success, had tried to engage me in conversation on the subject. Then he had resigned to join a fluidics group, whatever that was.

After a lonely dinner I went to bed. I slept for a couple of hours, then woke for a glass of water. Leaning across the bedside table I put on the light and fumbled around for my spectacles. As I did, I glanced at the carpet on the floor of the spacious room. It was a red carpet which was heavily patterned. But as I looked, it seemed as if the pattern was moving.

I couldn't make this out but eventually put my spectacles on. With horror, I saw that I was not looking at a pattern at all – the floor was covered in cockroaches rushing around in the unexpected light that now filled the room. Suddenly I was awake, very awake! The cockroaches disappeared rapidly, but I had lost all desire to sleep. I prayed, wondering whether cockroaches climbed the legs of beds. As I lay in bed, entirely awake, praying about both cockroaches and fluidic switches, I worked out what a fluidic switch must be. By morning I knew how to address the problem and eliminate it without any large-scale engineering alterations.

I got to the research site at 9 a.m. and the team assembled. At my request some further data were given to me. I did some calculations and, subject to some checks on the equipment, the problem was solved within thirty minutes. I later learned that, over the eleven years that it had been in existence, the laboratory had commissioned two teams of scientists to resolve the issue, without success.

There really is nothing that cannot be made a matter for prayer – though sometimes this may happen in unexpected ways. At times when God's people worship the Lord, for instance, he may be pleased to come and to heal and to restore.

We were at a camp for about a thousand people in the Lake District. There were plenty of fulfilling and exciting moments, none more so than one evening early on. The entire event was structured so that the conference delegates were in small groups, each led by a unit advisor, which was a kind of pastoral role. Of course, members of any unit soon formed a bond with each other. Elizabeth and I were advisors to an eclectic bunch of people which included a very quiet, unaccompanied sixteen-year-old girl. (Her friends belonged to another unit.) We were all rather protective of her since, while she would have been regarded as an attractive young lady, she had a problem: she was totally blind in one eye, having been bitten in the face by a dog some years before. The eye had since turned in its socket so much that the pupil and coloured iris could no longer be seen, leaving just the white of the eye on view.

As we filed towards the marquee there was an excitement in the air (just like we wish all church services had!) and this heightened expectation spilled over into the singing of a thousand voices. But then the sound changed. It swelled as shouting and a thrilled screaming could be heard from various sections of the vast congregation. The rumour spread like wildfire – people were being healed of physi-cal problems and medical conditions. The atmosphere was quite indescribable, and we realized that Jesus walked in our midst as we had never known before. Was this a form of mass hysteria, an uncontrolled emotion in which something primitive was being released from an assembly of people? Would we all settle down eventually and then feel rather embarrassed at our unseemly adolescent behaviour?

Well, we did settle down eventually. But we weren't embarrassed.

As we filed back to our units, it seemed that everyone was sharing a story breathlessly with anyone who would listen. Cocoa was dispensed and we stood in a circle. That was when I realized that our sixteen-year-old was not present. I finally spied her wending her way back to us. As she walked into the circle of bright light, our eyes fixed on her in blank astonishment. There was no doubt who it was – but she was different! It was the eye. No longer was it the ugly scar that made people look away. As she stood in front of me, a pair of perfect eyes looked at me, correctly aligned and with no disfiguring features. It was undeniable – her eye was whole.

Jesus had visited her as we had been singing, and he had done the miracle.

With the end of the camp we all went our various ways. Our sixteen-year-old went home to her religiously inclined mother who did not subscribe to anything her daughter might do. When the daughter came in, the mother was in the kitchen. She turned to greet her daughter. She saw her, eyes straight and sparkling as she smiled.

The mother screamed – and then fainted.

# 13.

# A Matter of Security

I have already explained how God made it very clear to me that he was interested in all of my life, including my professional work. It was not long, however, before I discovered that he wasn't the only one, as the governments of several countries came to regard my research as applicable to military aircraft.

As my speaking ministry grew, it inevitably took more time out of my working life, but the two continued to inform and enlighten each other. I didn't switch off my training in scientific enquiry to discuss the Christian life, nor did I file away any Christian thoughts so that I might grapple with the imponderables of engineering. After his death, it was said of Michael Faraday that it was impossible to know how to divide his thinking between the secular and the scientific – one merged into the other. And that can only occur if they do not contain contradictions with each other.

In fact, where there appeared to be conflict for me, my ultimate source of reference became the Bible. Yet clearly my Bible didn't actually say anything about magneto-hydrodynamics or fluid mechanics. Nevertheless, behind all that I was reading, expressed in the language of the day, lurked the two Laws of Thermodynamics.

Eventually, I resigned all of my academic and professional appointments in response to what I considered to be a direct call from God. It was a very difficult time but, with a mandatory three-month advance notice from my professional appointments, I was legally able to resign on one of just four days in any year, the quarter days.

At this point, I was a US Federal Government employee, my employers being the US Navy; but I was also directing a laboratory in the United Kingdom and acting as a consultant to several scientific and military bodies. All of those appointments had to be terminated. Then what was I to do? Colleagues in the Navy were kind enough to ensure that my office in California, the office facilities and my secretary, continued to be available to me, so for about three months I would go into my office in Monterey, California and, among other things, drink coffee from the machine conveniently placed at my office door!

The international Christian work began to grow quite rapidly, beginning with a series of meetings in Canada and expanding from that point. Soon a pleasing itinerary had built up, geographically focused on the West Coast of the United States, where I had been doing my scientific work. The itinerary grew from North America until invitations came from other countries, starting with France and followed by New Zealand soon after that.

Among this growing list came, at short notice, an invitation to speak at a conference in Strasbourg (at a congregation of 25,000!) and, at about the same time, an invitation to go to Lebanon. I had never been to Lebanon and was very interested in going. Without any solicitation by me, my air fare was guaranteed and, as discussions advanced, I learned that the senior officer of the US Marine Corps there was inviting me to address his troops in Beirut. They would be brought in from the field as duties allowed and my job was to tell them all about Jesus. I was so excited at the prospect that I resolved that nothing would deter me from this.

Arrangements were made to pick me up in Beirut and, as I understood it, go directly to the US military camp on the airport perimeter just a couple of minutes away. Just two days before I was to fly out from London's Heathrow airport, I spoke at a meeting in Guildford. It was a good meeting and I left feeling a measure of satisfaction for the evening, while looking forward to the coming visit to Lebanon. It was only a mile or so before turning on to the M25 that, to my total astonishment, I heard the Lord speak to me. He said, quite simply, that I was not to go.

'But, Lord, it's all arranged. I can't let people down.'

'Cancel the arrangements.'

'Lord, the tickets are paid for. I mustn't waste the money.'

'Cancel the arrangements – you are not to go.' The argument raged as the evening wore on. Initially I sat in a lay-by just before the motorway entrance, arguing with God. Then I travelled around the M25 and north along the M1, to arrive home knowing what I had to do, dreading it all.

I made the call. I was not popular but by now I knew that, for whatever reason, I must not go to Lebanon. The flight was cancelled, the visit to the Marine Base was cancelled, the itinerary was cancelled. I felt rotten. Two days later it was

October 23rd 1983 when I should have been on the flight. I still felt confused and quite unable to see the sense in what had been going on. What had the Lord been doing?

For those living in Beirut, that day in 1983 began with a familiar pattern of activity. Traffic was beginning in the city and especially around Beirut International Airport. At the airport perimeter nestled the headquarters of the US Military Mission to Lebanon, home to about 1,500 marines, the First Battalion of the Eighth Marines under the Second Marine Division. At 6.20 a.m. a water truck that was expected didn't arrive. Instead, a yellow Mercedes Benz truck followed by a second truck drove off the airport perimeter road and turned towards the US base. The guards at the gate, anticipating a water truck, were not to know that the vehicle approaching them had been high-jacked, nor were they aware that it was packed with explosives constructed as a gas-enhanced bomb consisting, it is thought, of a mixture of hexane, butane, propane and acetylene, together with conventional explosives.

The truck drove across the car park, then turned towards the perimeter, accelerating and crashing through the barbed-wire fence and between the sentry posts, before roaring through the gates, destroying them as it drove into the entrance hall of the building. It was here that the driver detonated his bomb – the equivalent of 12,000 pounds of TNT. The force of the explosion lifted the entire structure of the four-storey building off its foundations, shearing the support columns which were fifteen feet in circumference and strengthened by one-and-three-quarter-inch steel rods, before it crashed into a pile of rubble. In all, 241 American servicemen, 58 French servicemen and six civilians were killed, as well as the two suicide bombers.

The news flashed around the world. Seated in England I went cold as I heard the news, realizing that I was probably scheduled to be at the Marine headquarters that morning, maybe even at that time. Even if I hadn't been at the base at that precise moment, there is no doubt that the itinerary would have been severely compromised.

I began to realize that the Lord's hand was certainly on my life.

Any reader here would be excused for thinking that I would have learned my lesson through such dramatic circumstances. This was not the case, however. When I had cancelled the arrangements, I had made a promise that I would return to Lebanon and fulfil the itinerary. So now I set about fulfilling my word. A new trip was arranged and I was promised that every Protestant pastor in Lebanon would be present. They knew little about the work of the Holy Spirit, I was told, and I should go to teach on this subject.

Once more the dates were set and I was told of the preparations for the visit. I learned that a house had been prepared for my comfort, somewhere where peace and quiet could be guaranteed in an increasingly violent, disorganized country. The organizers admitted that things had got quite difficult in the country and there was an increase in lawlessness, but that it would be pretty safe in the areas I was to stay.

It must have been about four days before I was due to fly to Beirut that my quiet time was disturbed by the Lord speaking again to me: 'You are not to go. Cancel the arrangements.'

And so the arguments began again, but this time I knew that I should take more notice. And so I relented of my decision rather more easily, and phoned my contact in Beirut. There was no answer, so I rang again and at two-hour intervals over much of the next twenty-four hours. But it seemed that there was no way I could make contact with anyone in Lebanon. It was several days later that I received a phone call from Beirut.

'We couldn't call you because things have been very difficult. The war has broken out in our area. I could hear you calling but could not get to the phone. It's as well that you are not here. The house that was arranged for you has sustained a direct hit.'

Do I believe that God speaks to his people? Yes I do. Do I believe that when he speaks he says something? Absolutely. Do I believe that he can speak directly, meaningfully and specifically, seeing beyond the horizon of my knowledge and understanding? Yes I do. And to prove it I am alive to make this record.

The military interest in my work continued. Occasionally a student registered with me for what turned out to be not primarily academic reasons but in order to gain knowledge to assist his home nation's defence programme. One student went so far as to suggest that I become a consultant to his government (a lot of money was hinted at), then to inform me that the scientific attaché to his London embassy would be visiting me during the next week to 'discuss matters'. I had to move quickly to ensure I had 'a pressing engagement' elsewhere!

Even so, it didn't dawn on me where my scientific specialism was taking me until, one day, there was a knock on my office door and the Chief Security Officer for the Institute breezed in. We chatted about this and that and then he came to what was evidently the point of his visit.

'I hear that you're off to the Middle East next week.'

'Yes,' I said. 'I've been invited to give a paper at a scientific congress.'

'While you're there, could you do me a small favour?' It was to pass on a document to a friend of his. 'Don't bother to mention this to anyone. Actually, could you slip it into your other papers when you go through Customs?'

'What exactly is this document?' My mouth dropped as I learned that it was the complete flight stability performance envelope of the American F16 fighter – at that time still a highly secret combat aircraft.

'Do you have a diplomatic passport?' he continued. On hearing that I didn't, he said, 'There could be a real problem here. We wouldn't be able to get you out of the calaboose if you were picked up by their intelligence people. Maybe we should try a different approach. Are you good at remembering numbers?'

Now this went with the territory in my job, so without further ado I was given a series of digits and instructions to remember. I had inadvertently got so far into this I could find no way out.

'There's just one further thing. It's just possible that the CIA might latch on to you, so just be careful of anything you say if you don't know everyone around you.'

In due course, with Elizabeth as my companion, I caught the flight from Heathrow. Landing at our destination I looked through the window of the aircraft cabin to be greeted by the sight of heavily armed military personnel all around. If this was meant to offer security and comfort to the passengers, it failed in my case! (I was later to learn that all international flights were welcomed this way here.) The only instruction we had been given was to be available in our hotel room where we would be contacted.

The telephone call eventually came from a woman who instructed us to go to Tel Aviv and book into a particular hotel where we would be contacted again. This we did, while I wondered if I was still in the real world. Now quite certain that there were actual dangers with this job, I wished I had refused it. Was I praying about what was going on? You can bet on it!

The phone call came with the instruction to be in the foyer at 6 p.m. dressed for dinner. We would be picked up there.

Shortly before 6 p.m. we went to the reception area, sat down and waited. Apart from the girl on the desk there was no one about, so we sat in isolation while Elizabeth looked worried and I read the *Jerusalem Post*. It was just after 6 p.m. that Elizabeth, sitting bolt upright, said to me out of the corner of her mouth, 'Someone has just come through the main door.'

'That does happen in hotels,' I replied drily. Another silence, then more whispering: 'He's looking towards us! And now he's walking towards us.' Her whisper crept up the scale, then I heard a man's voice: 'Peacock?'

'Yes,' I responded.

'Follow me, please.'

As we stepped out of the hotel door, a very large limousine slid up, the doors opened and we were ushered in. We drove out of Tel Aviv into the night, Elizabeth and I in the back seat, our contact seated next to the driver. Another passenger sat in the tail of the car. He didn't speak at all.

Eventually, after climbing through a range of hills, we reached a compound defined by high walls on which there was a generous distribution of barbed wire. The gates opened ahead of us as we arrived, and we swept in. Within a few seconds we arrived at the front door of a house.

'Stay here please,' said our contact, 'and don't get out of the car. The guard dogs are loose – and dangerous!' We stayed in the car.

Eventually, the front door of the house opened and we were welcomed into a beautifully furnished and elegant building. The walls were covered in paintings. Among these I noticed a Picasso, and it wasn't a print. The very large sitting room was filled with couples, all very well dressed, chatting in amiable fashion. After introductions we were led into the dining room where animated if inconsequential discussions took us through the several courses. On one side sat a lady who was a gemologist and made fabulously expensive jewellery. Adjacent was another lady, the wife of our host, who had recently 'popped over to London to see a couple of shows'. Then, of course, there were the men – polite and generous in nature, but far more serious.

I was bemused by the whole event, feeling totally out of place in this company and these surroundings. It became evident that my host had a lively interest in the arms industry. He appeared to be the Minister of Defence for his country, while the other men were, in the main, people who worked for him in one capacity or another.

While no direct questions were being asked, I eventually realized that the assembly was trying to find out everything about me, in particular the nature and details of my research programme. The ladies having been led to an ante-room, there were about eight men left until, time advancing, one stood to say that he must be leaving. That was the trigger for everyone to excuse themselves, so very soon there were just three of us left in the room. This included the silent passenger in our car on the way to the evening dinner.

Conversation dragged a little until, looking quite uncomfortable, the silent man finally spoke. 'May I use your washroom?' he asked, and was directed down the hallway. At last my host was alone. This was my chance.

'I have a message for you and it's from Bill Agnew.'

'Ah, yes. I've been waiting for this.' I delivered the message, carefully memorized, including the list of numbers.

'Thanks for that,' he said, writing the information down and folding the sheet into his pocket just as the door opened and our shadow returned.

Our host said he would like to join us in the lengthy journey back to Tel Aviv. As it turned out, I was glad he did.

So far as I could judge, we were driving off a range of hills and were somewhere in the region of the foot of the Golan Heights, when lights were flashed in the road ahead, signalling us to stop. We came to a halt and the driver opened the window. Outside stood a vigilante of some type. He thrust a gun through the opening and began cross-examining the driver. The car was surrounded by young men, all carrying AK-47 rifles. The questioning continued, the driver's answers clearly not proving satisfactory.

At this point our host, who had been sitting quietly, was galvanized into action. Speaking quietly but authoritatively in the local language, he apparently told the fellow to put his gun down. When the gun remained pointing at us in the car, our host lost his temper. He shouted at the gunman and added some invective to press his point home.

Elizabeth and I remained silent witnesses to the unfolding drama, fairly close to terror level. What on earth had I done to get us into this mess? I had simply agreed to do a colleague a favour. I had brought my wife into countries about which we knew nothing, among total strangers, and had put us in a potentially lethal situation over which I had no control. Prayer was never more desperate.

As our host shouted at our captors, they jumped back from the car and the guns were lowered. Evidently they had discovered who our travelling companion was.

I felt tremendous relief when I saw that AK-47 being withdrawn from the window. We listened to one or two more brief exchanges and then we were waved on our way. As we drove through the night we could make out a number of mobile guards, all in high-speed vehicles with mounted machine guns, rushing up and down the coastline.

With relief unabated we eventually found ourselves back in our hotel and, with yet greater relief, on an El-Al flight to London the very next day.

Heart-stopping as it all was, the Lord had amply demonstrated that he was able to keep his hand on our lives, irrespective of the danger levels we faced.

It was at about this time that I was invited to give a paper at a conference in San Francisco. It was my first visit, memorable for staying at a hotel in Union Square in the heart of the downtown area. For breakfast on my first morning there I ordered a blueberry high-stack, eager to find out what it was. It was unbelievable. On the plate before me was a column of eight pancakes, all interleaved with very large portions of blueberry sauce. As a modest egg and bacon man I thought I might die! I survived.

Later that morning, while walking off the pancakes around the square's periphery, I was surprised to see a man walking purposefully out of a side street and straight towards me. At a distance of about seven yards he took a revolver from his pocket, lifted it and pointed it at me. With horror I saw his finger tighten on the trigger. There was no time to react in any way, so I watched as I saw the gun jam without releasing its charge. I kept walking – briskly – although a man walking on the pavement close by, who had seen the whole event, went white, clutched at his heart and croaked, 'O my God,' before falling over in shock. For my part, I continued walking – quickly. After all, I said to myself using my best British reserve, we haven't been introduced!

If I ever needed confirmation that God was interested in me, here it was. God was clearly able to control any event. Twice now I had looked down the barrel of a gun, even once seen the gunman pull the trigger, and on neither occasion had a shot been fired. Both times I manifestly had no control over the situation.

I needed no further convincing that the God I served was in total control. He is the God who holds a personal and dedicated interest in his people and their wellbeing. There will be those who ask, 'But what about the people who die in catastrophes? What about those who die for their faith every day? Are you telling me that God's care doesn't extend to the likes of those – only to you?'

And the only answer I can give is that God, whom we know through a personal relationship with Jesus, deals with us as individuals at a personal level. I can neither know the detailed personal circumstances of these people, nor can I adjudicate on what God should do. That, frankly, is his domain. It is his prerogative to set his hand to whatever he thinks best.

# 14.

# A Full Itinerary

Over time I became uneasy as I observed my professional work begin to be shoe-horned around opportunities for Christian ministry. This did not present a problem while I was in the UK, but as the ministry spread to other countries I recognized the impossibility of combining a Christian itinerary with a diary of professional commitments.

Thinking about this problem, I was ashamed to identify in myself a hidden motive attached to what I was doing when I was abroad. I was actually less than sure about the certainty of my calling, and so I had come to rely on a fall-back position in the event of things going wrong. I knew I could always say, 'Actually I'm a scientist over here on business – always happy to talk about my faith.' Then, if someone didn't like what I was doing, I could just walk away from the Christian meetings and get on with the real commitments in my life – the pursuit of science.

This was a major challenge. Could I face up to the possibility of undertaking Christian speaking commitments in a completely separate itinerary, without my safety net? I knew that I must, or this increasingly exciting and demanding Christian life would simply wither on the vine.

My first visit to New Zealand was a very surprising event. While I was speaking in the Mojave Desert in North America I was asked by a man whether I would go to New Zealand.

I explained that I had no connections in that country and wouldn't go without an invitation. When he pressed me I said that I would come if he made all the arrangements – and then thought nothing more about it. So I was surprised when an invitation to do a national tour arrived on my desk.

Things did not begin well. Flying from England I stopped overnight in Los Angeles to see some friends and finished up speaking at a meeting. The meeting went so well that, in the excitement, I left my Bible on the piano. This I discovered the next day while somewhere over the Pacific Ocean. Thus I arrived in Auckland, Bible-less, thirteen hours disorientated, to meet people I had never met and knew nothing about.

At the airport I was met by a very gentle and loving man with a Scots accent and taken to his home where I arrived around seven o'clock in the morning. It was here that my host for the itinerary, Bill, would meet me. Having learned a little about New Zealand, I asked the Scottish gentleman where we would find the revival. 'In the UK' was his encouraging response!

At 9 a.m. the front door bell rang. I could see from my seat in the living room that two men had arrived. Then the Lord spoke to me. 'The one on your left is Bill; the one on the right will give you trouble.' I had never heard anything like this before. Could God speak in such terms and with such precision? I decided to be ready for anything.

'Roy, let me introduce Bill who has put together this invitation. And this is Greg, who is an associate of Bill's and

runs some of the churches that Bill leads around the nation.'
We talked amiably and then Bill referred matters to Greg
who would go over the three-month programme. Greg had
not spoken so far.

We entered Greg's office, a few yards away on the other
side of a compound of domestic buildings, sat down and
faced each other. Greg began with a frontal assault, 'Who
sent you here?' he asked. I gave a non-committal answer but
Greg was not to be easily satisfied. 'I want to know by whose
authority you have come to New Zealand.'

'Greg, I know what you're getting at. You want me to be
able to say that I have been commissioned by a church. I
can't give you that assurance, since my church in England
isn't into that sort of structure. What I can do, however, is
say that I am here on the authority of Jesus.'

Greg fumed and then turned to the business of my itinerary. 'You are to have two days rest to re-orientate and then
I've arranged a meeting in three days' time at Whangarei
where you're speaking to a church. The next day you're travelling on to Kerikeri for the Sunday service in a church there
and then you will be returning to Auckland for a meeting at
our church sometime.

'And then?' I asked.

'That's it,' was the reply.

'Let me get this straight,' I said. 'You have invited me
to New Zealand for a three-month itinerary, for which I
have just flown 13,000 miles, and then there will be another
13,000 miles to get back to the UK, and the itinerary
consists of three meetings. Do I hear you correctly?'

'That is what I have arranged.'

'Do you reckon that this is reasonable behaviour – to bring me half way around the world to speak for a total of about two hours?'

'Listen,' Greg hissed at me. 'If God wants you here, he will arrange the itinerary.' At that he turned, stamped out and I was left alone in a country in which I knew no one.

There was worse was to come. Two days later I was driven to the Auckland Bus Station to get a seat on a coach to Whangarei. I then realized that I had no New Zealand currency, although I didn't share this lack with anyone. My Scots driver asked me to stay in the car while he went into the bus station and I sat there wondering how I was going to find the money for my ticket. A few minutes later my driver returned and pushed something into my hand. It was a ticket to Whangarei.

'How did you know that I had no currency?' I asked.

'Oh, God told me as we were driving down.' So God was on the case. I took comfort.

I was taken straight to the meeting in Whangarei where it was clear that a congregation had been drummed up – folk who clearly had better things to do with themselves that evening. Speaking was like dropping lead bricks over the lectern. Eventually the meeting drew mercifully to a close. Folk milled around, everyone avoiding me, so I approached my host who had convened the meeting to enquire where I was staying that night.

'You are with John and Anne. They farm about fifteen miles north and they will take you on to Kerikeri tomorrow.'

We drove to the farmhouse in silence, John at the wheel, Anne in the back seat, and me in the front passenger seat. I was fed up, plotting secretly how I might change my flight ticket and flee back to the UK. My hosts seemed fed up too, doubtless unamused by the prospect of putting me up and getting me through the next sector of my triumphal progress through the nation. But it was in the silence of those moments that the Lord spoke to me.

'I'm going to heal this woman.' The words were delivered in an unmistakable manner.

'Why, what is wrong with her, Lord?'

'I shall heal her.' I was convinced that this was going to happen, but what should I do? I stole a glance over my shoulder to see if there was something observably wrong with her. She looked perfectly normal.

We arrived at the farmhouse and retired quickly – a relief after a disastrous evening.

The next morning we had breakfast in silence and then my hosts prepared for the long drive. John went to the garage to get his car out. I was alone with Anne and decided that now would be the only opportunity I might have to raise the subject of her health.

'Do you enjoy good health?' I asked cautiously.

'Yes.'

'Are you in good health just now?'

Again, the positive response was no encouragement to me.

'Do you have any pain at all?'

'No.' I was getting nowhere so, in my heart, I cried out to God, 'You're going to have to tell me what her problem is, Lord.'

'Her right leg is shorter than her left by one inch.' Now I had something to go on.

'Do you ever get pain in the lower part of the back?' Yes, she did. Never have I been so overjoyed that someone was in pain.

'Do you have it now?' Again she did, so I said to her, 'I believe that you have one leg shorter than the other. In fact, I think that it is the right leg that is short,' and I realized, too late, that I was being boxed into a corner. The dreadful consequences could already be seen in my eyes when I was rescued in the nick of time by John's return.

'John,' I blurted out, 'I believe that the Lord has told me that Anne has one leg shorter than the other, and that he wants to restore the parity of the legs, getting rid of her back pain.' John clearly thought that I was barking mad, but there was no going back.

'We can compare the length of her legs, John,' I stumbled on, adding hastily, 'There's nothing to be concerned over. She doesn't even need to raise her skirt. In fact . . .' – by now I was pouring out my thoughts as quickly as I could before he did some damage to me – '. . . you could support her legs, lifting them to the horizontal position and holding them there while we pray. And then the Lord will grow the short leg.'

John had to do something, so he held his wife's legs in a horizontal attitude. Sure enough, the right leg was shorter than the left one by about an inch. We prayed – and nothing happened. I continued to pray, and then Anne let out a scream: 'I can feel it growing!' And, sure enough, we could see it growing. Over a period of less than a minute the leg grew until both Anne's legs coincided in length. God had done the work, Anne had testified to feeling a leg grow, John was just flabbergasted – and I was not a little relieved!

In due course, Anne went off to pack her bag while John and I waited. Eventually, I asked John how long Anne would be.

'I don't know,' he rejoined, with customary husbandly resignation. 'Right now she's on the phone calling all her friends between here and Kerikeri to tell them what God has just done.'

Eventually we set off, Anne looking like the cat that got the cream, me trying to look composed, and John still trying to get his head around what he had just witnessed.

Sunday morning came and, with it, a crowd that filled the building. The place was packed, the stage was filled with various dignified people and the level of expectation was clearly high.

Just as I rose to speak, the Lord gave me a word for two sicknesses present. Now, this put me into a quandary. By now in my Christian walk I had read all the relevant Scriptures to guide me in this area and seen many acted out before my eyes. So far as I was concerned, the Holy Spirit gave the word for healing at the end of the address, not the beginning!

I wrestled with this for a while, then spoke out what I felt was a word from God. After all, I reasoned, God was quite capable of healing someone at any point in a service, not just when we determined it should be. I said that the person involved had no need to respond for all to see: they should just receive from God. One could not digest solids and had to have their food put through a mixer first; and the second was someone with a serious eye condition. To avoid any misunderstanding, I mentioned again that the recipients need not answer in an open manner: God had healed them.

When the service finished, the pastor asked me to stand at the door to greet people as the congregation filed out. Among the last was a short, middle-aged lady and, by way of being pleasant, I asked her if she normally came to this church.

'Oh no,' came her emphatic reply, 'I only came because I heard that you would be here. You see, I was going to ask you to pray for my aged mother.'

'We could do that right now,' I encouraged her.

'There's no point,' she rejoined. 'My Mum has been healed.'

'Really. Why do you say that?'

'My mother has not been able to eat solid foods for a very long time, so all her food goes through the mixer. But not only that. Her eyesight has deteriorated so much that she is now virtually blind: she can't read the writing on a page. But I believe that those words were for her as well.'

Standing in the porch of the building we prayed together for her mum.

I later learned that, when the lady walked through the front door of her home, she heard her mother call from her bedroom. 'Come in here – there's something I want to say.' Then she heard her mother say, 'I'm fed up with eating all that muck. Get me a proper roast dinner. I want roast potatoes, cabbage and a joint of lamb!' The daughter complied and then watched as her mother, incapable of eating solid foods, enjoyed her first proper Sunday lunch in years. Then, to cap things off, she proceeded to read the Sunday newspaper.

Soon they were on the phone telling the old lady's granddaughter in Auckland all about it. She listened in wonder and then asked her mother who this visiting speaker was.

'It was some fellow from England. I think that his name was Peacock.'

'Mum . . . you don't know this, but my boss had the job of arranging his itinerary in New Zealand – and he didn't bother to do it. The papers have been left on my desk. I'll tell you what I'll do. Tomorrow, when I get into the office, I'm going to telephone churches all over the nation.'

One day later I had a full itinerary for New Zealand, organized out of the office of the man whose original responsibility it had been.

On a subsequent visit to New Zealand I was able to spend some time with the indigenous Maori population. My schedule was to include Taumarunui, a pretty town on the banks of the largest lake in the nation (and with the most outstanding stock of fish, all lurking around waiting to be caught).

One of my commitments was to speak to a group of Maori women. Twelve were present, so the event was closer to a chat than an address. At one point, however, I felt that I heard the Lord tell me to pray for a blood condition which he described.

Not being a medical man, this was going to be one of those moments when the heart is in the mouth and the speaker is shiftily looking for the door marked 'Exit' to facilitate a quick getaway! Considering the number present, I didn't need to do a statistical analysis to know that the probability of that precisely defined illness being present was remote.

Nevertheless, I spoke the word, hoping against hope that maybe one person would respond. I tried to look composed but, frankly, I was speechless when seven of the dozen present responded and presented themselves for prayer.

Checking up on this medical condition some time later, I learned from an informed source that what I had described was a known blood condition, but that it was very rare and was only carried by one known ethnic group in the world – the Maoris.

# 15.

# New Life the Dead Receive

The period in history known as the Renaissance ushered in new expressions of art and architecture that have affected us ever since and led to a philosophical and intellectual development that we now call the Enlightenment. This too has changed many of our ways of thinking. The nineteenth-century German philosopher, Immanuel Kant, defined the Enlightenment as an age shaped by the Latin motto, *sapere aude* – 'dare to know'. Kant was anxious that people should be set free from the burden of traditional thinking from the past. He wanted them to have the courage to make use of their own understanding, without recourse to another authority.

Now, I for one have reason to be grateful for the sort of liberty in thinking that this philosophy affords. Without it science would never make advances. But Kant never defined a starting point for his thinking, nor thought it even necessary to mention that one may exist. Yet the truth is, we do not live in such a void.

In fact our lives are shaped not by developing abstract thoughts and philosophies but by the world with which we interact. Now when we discover contradictions between our philosophy and our experience, it is necessary that experience win the day. Our thinking is altered to accommodate our experience. So, while it is natural enough to reject a supposed event that does not fit with our philosophy (like a miracle), the challenge comes when the event becomes an experience. And that is what happened to me.

I was an atheist not because of any conviction, but because I had found nothing to contradict that position. As we have seen, my exposure to religion had done little more than lead me to read the prayers in the correct manner and sing in tune as required. It was into this void that the Christian message made its invasion.

When, therefore, I found friends and acquaintances who looked for and found a personal God, it was a source of wonder to me. That people could have their lives changed in this manner impressed me beyond measure. Further, when we discovered that prayer meant something, that situations and people could be changed, that too was a marvel. In the earliest days of my Christian life I heard a recording of a woman giving a testimony in which her opening statement was, 'I don't know what prayer is. I only know that it is.' In simple terms, that has remained my position ever since.

But my training in the scientific method led me to observe a connection between prayers and results. What that connection was precisely – in physical, relational or mechanical terms – I did not know. Yet it was there.

When I started to look for guidance in my life, it was a tremendous joy to be able to pray and know that God would answer.

But there was a huge challenge when it came to the matter of physical healing – one we all share to some degree. Even if I could accommodate the idea of God, conveniently remote in his fastness in heaven; even if I believed that he could hear my prayer and do something about it; nevertheless the thought that he might come down from heaven to visit me, maybe touch my body and heal me, was quite frankly rather frightening.

Yet the scientist in me could not ignore or refute the evidence. I have been aware over the years of the arguments of detractors – I am mistaken, I am deluded, the event has been misreported, it's all psychosomatic, it's nonsense, it's a con, it's not scientific.

Sometimes a detractor will look for surer ground. 'Okay,' he says, 'you talk of people being healed. It's one thing to report people being healed of sick headaches, toothache, rheumatics and so on; but I'll guarantee you've never seen anyone being raised from the dead. There's the test. Yes, there are reports of people being raised from the dead in Jesus' day, but that is history – and in any case we can't be sure at this distance in time that the record is faithful. Today, the facts are quite simple: people are not raised from the dead.'

But is that right?

It was about a year after my conversion that I went to the local church for the Sunday evening service. The congregation was just a dozen or so, and the minister led us, professionally and flawlessly, through the pages of the book until we arrived at the series of prayers reserved for the moment. The mellifluous tones as his voice was raised and lowered were sharply interrupted by a rather strangled noise coming from the congregation. This was followed by a thud as a body hit the ground. The minister stopped and looked around in irritation that his words had been interrupted. There was a very short pause – only a second or so – as a couple of sidesmen dragged the body of the parishioner away from the pews.

The minister finished the list of prayers, evidently satisfied that the situation had been redeemed. And so the service continued, almost seamlessly.

I was appalled. The man's health and, as I learned later, his life were in danger, yet all that seemed to matter was that the rites of the service had been meticulously observed. Ironically the interrupted prayer was labelled in the book 'Prayer for the Sick'!

This incident left an indelible memory – and a question: how do we in the church respond to the sick who need prayer? And, *in extremis*, what can we do about someone who is thoughtless enough to die during a service?

Visiting the Channel Islands has always been a particular pleasure. Not only are they beautiful islands, the people are warm-hearted and the flights are a particular joy – especially years ago when we flew in a small aircraft with twin engines that made a lot of noise and vibration. For me, this was 'Biggles' stuff from another age. (To make the experience complete, I felt that passengers really should have been issued with leather flying helmets and goggles along with their boarding passes.)

The itinerary in Jersey included a speaking engagement in a large church-building in St Helier. On the Sunday morning the pews were full. The local scout troop was there presenting colours at the beginning of the proceedings. It was a warm, happy and quite noisy service. At one point, as I was sitting facing the congregation, I noticed a slight disturbance. One or two people in the last-but-one row at the back were leaning over and standing up and leaning over again. Then the door at the rear of the church opened and two men in uniforms I didn't recognize (but wrongly assumed were part of the scout troop) rushed in, picked up a body which I had not previously seen from the floor, put it on a stretcher and carried it out.

As the service continued, someone stepped up to the minister and whispered in his ear and then, while the congregation sang, the minister stepped over to whisper in my ear.

'I should tell you that there has been a problem with a long-standing member of the congregation who, you may have noticed, collapsed earlier. He was taken to hospital but unfortunately has now died. Before you speak, I will make an announcement to the church, we will pray and sing an extra hymn. Then maybe you will speak to us.'

What does one do in the circumstances? The address I had prepared seemed particularly unsuitable so, praying in desperation, I mentally tore up my notes and asked the Lord to give me the word for the moment.

He did.

My focus was on the choice we have to respond to God, with the clear and unavoidable consequence of heaven or hell. Which should it be? Life was short and uncertain: today was the day to resolve matters.

Our heads were bowed, the challenge was made – and the response was beyond my wildest dreams. A queue of people came forward, a significant proportion of the congregation, and counselling went on for a very long time after that.

That day I had learned a lesson. But was there more than this surrounding a death among believers?

It is difficult to imagine a more unlikely place to see a memorable work of God than in the shopping centre of Bedford in England. This is an area with a series of inter-secting walkways and arcades with retail shops throughout and a small square which consequently has a lot of pedes-trian traffic. A few people are often to be seen there, sitting on a dwarf wall, taking a moment's rest in the exertions of a shopping trip. One or two might have a sandwich on which to munch as they admire the post-war architecture.

As Elizabeth and I crossed this area while shopping one day, I noticed a couple walking ahead of me. The man was tall, fairly well built and in his sixties. His wife was a much shorter person and quite slight in comparison. I noticed that the man was not walking in a straight line. As he staggered along, his wife tried to support him, but his knees began to buckle. The wife cried out and several people close by rushed towards them. One person ran into a shop to bring out a chair. By now the woman had got her husband to a shop doorway, but he couldn't aim himself accurately and he collapsed on to the chair that was hastily pushed beneath him.

By now he had lost consciousness. His breathing quickly became irregular, he gasped, and from his throat came a rattling noise. I had read about the death rattle but had never heard it and actually believed it was a figment of a writer's fertile imagination. It wasn't. I heard it!

Several of us stood in a circle, looking on in horror, realizing what we had just witnessed.

The man's wife was beside herself with grief. She was crying uncontrollably, holding his hand, ignoring the crowd who looked on helplessly. And then she did the only thing she knew how. She cried out, 'O God, help us!'

There was a pause while she was overcome by the moment, then once more, 'O God, help us.' This was repeated once more and then there was a further pause.

'O Lord, help us!' I couldn't help noticing the change from 'God' to 'Lord'.

At that moment, as we all looked on, we saw the most astonishing thing. The man's chest began to lift up and down. Then his eyes flickered and opened. In a few minutes he was sitting up alongside his wife, as a mystified but evidently satisfied audience of shoppers quietly walked away.

As I turned to go, a lady from the crowd touched my arm and explained that she was a nurse, a matron in fact, at the Bedford General Hospital, South Wing. She was as astounded as any of us. 'I watched that man,' she said. 'He was dead! I know it – he was dead.'

What had brought the remarkable change in these tragic circumstances? That I will never know for sure, but I certainly couldn't avoid noticing that change in the woman's language. Like many people caught up in a tragedy like this, she had cried out 'O God!' These are words that can be used in almost any manner – from blaspheming, through a general cry to an unknown deity, to worship of the living God. Had God been distant to her before, some kind of lucky charm perhaps? I don't know. But it did appear that, as 'God' became 'Lord', the 'very present help in trouble' (Psalm 46:1) was right there with her, to intervene on her behalf and deal with the situation. This God, who sticks closer than a brother (see Proverbs 18:24), was there to act. And at her cry of commitment and total dependence, that is what he did.

This was not the only time I saw the Lord move to bring someone back from the dead. During my first visit to New Zealand my itinerary took me to the north-east of North Island and the Coromandel Peninsula, a modestly populated and beautiful region where I was to speak at a church. I will always remember that it was next door to the local fire station. I mentioned to the pastor that we were clearly fully prepared in the event that the Holy Spirit fell in fire on the church! Little did I know what would actually transpire.

The time came for me to speak. Before long I was in top gear and enjoying things in a relaxed manner. That was when, right before me, a heart-stopping moment occurred. In the middle of the front row an older man suddenly let out a loud groan, made as if to stand, and then fell over to his left, clutching his chest.

The service stopped in its tracks and people began to crowd round to help in any way they could. There seemed little point – he showed all the signs of having died. One or two supported his body and gently laid him out on the floor, while the quiet voices of a praying congregation filled the place. No one – least of all me – knew what to do. But then, after we had been standing around for several minutes feeling totally helpless, the wife of the pastor spoke aloud with a voice full of authority that filled the building: 'Spirit of death, I command you to go – now!'

We were all taken aback, me especially. I had been staying at the home of the pastor and his wife for two or three days. She was clearly a quiet lady – in fact I don't recall having previously heard her voice. So this came as a total surprise.

But that was as nothing to what happened next. The inert body moved. It began breathing, the eyes flickered and opened and, with the enthusiastic support of the congregation, the man was brought up to a sitting position before standing shortly afterwards.

Before we left there was a curious 'action replay' of the incident in Bedford, as a lady once more took me aside to say, 'I'm a nursing sister in the local hospital, and I know a dead body when I see one. There is no doubt in my mind that he was dead.'

So what have I learned from all this?

It seems to me that the Lord is entirely capable of doing anything he chooses. If, in the matter of physical healing, he is able to reveal his power in dealing with the ultimate challenge of the 'last enemy' (1 Corinthians 15:26), there is nothing that is beyond him.

In scientific terminology, these events in Bedford and New Zealand demonstrate a violation of the Second Law of Thermodynamics. In short, these are miracles.

Over the bridge of two hundred years I hear the voice of Immanuel Kant saying, 'It is beyond a doubt that all our knowledge begins with experience.' Kant clearly valued experience as one of the most desirable qualities. To interpret this quotation, he drives the conclusion that, unless we have the experience, we do not have the knowledge. If this is the case, it should be our personal responsibility to gain experience of God and his ways, so that our knowledge of God may not be a theoretical fancy but a real, life-changing aspect of our existence.

It is on this basis that we should approach the subject of miracles of healing, even the raising of the dead. I am cautious in receiving and handling data, as a scientist should be. It is part of my remit to collate any set of data and form a reasoned conclusion that reflects the evidence contained in those data. So how am I to have the knowledge of such outstanding works of God? It is by gaining the experience.

Over a bridge of three thousand years I hear another voice – a poet-philosopher and warrior-king called David, making a similar appeal to experience: 'O taste and see that the LORD is good' (Psalm 34:8).

I must taste and then I will see – and what I see, I for one will report. After all, that's what scientists do.

# 16.

# What Does the Lord Require?

Growth in the Christian way of life has never, for me, been a matter of reading a how-to book and then emulating what the book has taught me. Recalling the time that Elizabeth and I went to Trafalgar Square in London, we were young Christians, not versed in the Bible and having no experience of what we were about to be immersed in. We didn't even know where to find a book to cover our subject. We were cast upon the one certainty we had discovered in those earliest days – our relationship with Jesus Christ.

I had plenty of experience in my chosen field of science but it seemed that the only thing I could rely upon for the spiritual realm was that, when some quite fundamental scientific axioms were added up, they assured me this was Mission Impossible!

We had some thinking to do, since it was apparent that we had touched, almost inadvertently, on something no one had ever told us. If the potential was there to see lives changed, not only in becoming Christians but in being healed, why was it that nobody ever talked about it?

And why was it that, while I learned of the God who loved me, I was not encouraged to believe that his personal interest stretched as far as my working life?

I seemed to be discovering the Christian life the hard way.

But I was discovering something else that even now does not fail to confuse me. Elizabeth and I had become part of a church where, it seemed, not every member believed Christ, or if they did, it was only so far as was convenient. For them Christianity must not be challenging, and consequently we were obliged to ignore those areas in the Jesus story which stood a chance of confronting anything or anybody. Sermons were preached in the third person since anything more direct might offend. Other than as a theoretical possibility, we were not actually to believe that Jesus was capable of bringing people into new life – to change their lives. Least of all should we believe that he could change our situations, our plans, our friends and family, or our bodies.

That said, I had my own lessons to learn in the ways of God.

One evening I was driving into Consett in County Durham, looking for a farmhouse where I was to stay overnight before travelling on to an early morning meeting. Looking for farmhouses in the dead of night is not one of my strong points, so it took a while, but when I found it I did wonder why since all the lights in the place were on. It turned out that my hosts for the evening had decided to have a party to welcome me. The house was jam-packed with happy Christians. All I wanted to do was go to bed!

I dropped my bag in my room, gazed longingly at the bed, then went down to the junketings. It was some hours before I could find an excuse to slip away. Exhausted, I unpacked my overnight bag, laid out my clothes for the next day, undressed and reached for my pyjamas. Just as I got to that moment of inherent instability as, balanced on one leg, I tried to locate the other trouser leg with my foot, a voice spoke clearly to me: 'What doth the Lord require of thee?' I was so shocked and disorientated that I lost my balance and fell over on to the bed, one leg entwined and one still free. Still, I listened intently, realizing that God had spoken to me. I knew these words were somewhere in the Bible, though I had no idea where.

Reaching for my Hebrew *Gesenius* (which, along with my Thayer's Greek-English lexicon, I always had with me when travelling), I began the hunt and soon found the reference:

> And what doth the LORD require of thee, but to do justly, and to love mercy, and to walk humbly with thy God? (Micah 6:8)

I read this again and again, with growing horror as I heard the enquiry turned into an indictment. All weariness now evaporated as I sat on the bed examining my heart before the Lord. This was not an ambition I had heard, a request or suggestion that there could be a slight trimming of the sails, a re-ordering of things to make God happy; this was a requirement. And I realized that a requirement from God was not to be ignored.

I looked at these three aspects of life as expressed in the quotation: justice, mercy and humility.

As best I knew how, I always behaved with justice. The team of scientists who worked for me seemed to think so, and it would not have been possible to run a team of scientists any other way.

Mercy was, I decided, used wherever there was a call for it. Introducing young scientists to the new disciplines of working in a team involved the application of mercy, especially in the correcting of faults.

But humility? My training at school had been in a competitive atmosphere, the sports we played were competitive, the studies we undertook were with a view to gaining top marks in the class and then being sure that the remainder of the class knew about it. In the way that it worked out, I could see there was no encouragement towards humility.

There was one piece of poetry from Victorian England that had had an enormous effect on me as a child. It was called *Vitaï Lampada* ('The Torch of Life' written by Henry Newbolt in 1897) and it contained this immortal verse:

And it's not for the sake of a ribboned coat,
Or the selfish hope of a season's fame,
But his Captain's hand on his shoulder smote:
'Play up! play up! and play the game!'

It was a sentiment that I had set aside in a competitive world. Yet the picture had a resonance with me. I have to admit that, coming from a cricketing family, I longed for the sort of success portrayed by Newbolt and Kipling and others, and the smell of freshly cut grass and linseed oil has never failed to excite me. And so, lurking in my memory, there was this verse to remind me that competition can be selfless. This was something that was going to be a big call for me (and it always has been), but I knew I had to work on it.

I got off the bed, managed to get my pyjamas on, and fell quickly into a deep sleep for the couple of hours that remained of this night.

Clearly I still had much to learn.

Ontario in Canada has always been a delightful place to visit and, as it turned out, a great location in which I might learn the things of God. My first visit was as a guest of the Canadian government. A PhD student of mine was in the military, and a number of invitations to speak came from Christian organizations.

I soon realized that my visits could not include both scientific and Christian itineraries at the same time. It all came to a head during a flight to Toronto. I was reading a Canadian newspaper. Having worked my way through the headline stories, I was now reading the minor articles and then the adverts (it was a long flight). You may understand my astonishment when I saw my name dominating one of the advertisements. Readers were encouraged to come and hear me at a large venue in the city of Toronto and were left in no doubt that they would be hearing from Jesus. I read this with horror and distress, sensing the embarrassment to scientists and government officials whom I was also scheduled to meet while in Canada.

As it happened, the entire scientific establishment of Canada omitted to read the advert – either that or they were too polite to mention anything in my hearing.

It was a full schedule in Toronto, beginning with an early morning breakfast meeting with Christian businessmen. I then had to find the next venue. I was driving at fairly high speed along an elevated carriageway when I had a mortifying thought: I hadn't actually planned what I was going to talk about. Up to then addresses had always been carefully arranged affairs – my notes, while in compressed form, always covered what I was to say quite fully. There had even been a time, early on, when I had kept all of my notes carefully filed but, as Elizabeth correctly predicted, I never went back to them. On this occasion, I had been so busy organizing my thoughts for the breakfast meeting that I had completely forgotten about this one. I was driving headlong to a meeting, at which I would be speaking for about an hour to four hundred people, with no clue what I should be talking about.

I prayed. Fervently. 'What am I supposed to be speaking on, Lord?'

The miles ticked away very quickly. 'O Lord, what should I be speaking on? Even one word would do right now!'

And then, to my considerable surprise, God spoke to me, just one word. 'Faith.' Well, that was one word, but maybe he could give me another to go with it. But that was all that came. I had asked for one word and I had got it. How was I to handle this? How could I stand before an audience of four hundred people and speak just one word?

In my desperation I prayed once more. 'Lord, if I speak that one word, I will believe you to give me the rest of the address as I speak.'

I arrived at the front entrance to the large assembly hall just in time, where I was met by a small team of relieved organizers who had been worried that I might not make it. I noticed they were all women. I was led into the hall where I was astonished to find an audience of four hundred women. I had never done this before, and I was terrified. And, as if that were not frightening enough, I had just one word to speak.

At the appropriate moment I rose to my feet and croaked out my one word: 'Faith.' As soon as I did so, the whole of my message came flooding in. I relaxed as I saw the shape, structure and content of the address framing up before me. It seemed that, as well as talking about faith, I was learning about it – a lesson that came not from a book but from stepping out and doing it. This was experimental Christianity at its most basic – raw, uncooked and certainly not pre-digested.

I had spoken for about an hour when God spoke to my heart. It was a word for a woman I took to be in the audience. 'There is a lady here,' I said, 'who has a medical condition which I can describe in these terms. It is a serious condition.' I went on to describe the condition and then announced, 'You do not need to come forward but the Lord heals you where you are now. In the name of Jesus, be healed.'

The service concluded a couple of minutes later, the time was just twelve o'clock, and lunch with the organizers beckoned. As people were milling around, one of the organizers spoke to me. 'It was such a pity,' she said. 'You see, I know the lady that word was intended for. It's Julie from our group. You described her medical condition exactly. But the pity is this, she isn't here today. She regularly comes to our meetings but she had an appointment with her physician today. Oh, I feel so sad because I've no doubt that the word was for her.'

One of the great advantages of being a guest at a ladies meeting is that there is always a remarkable feast laid on. Lunch was, in this instance, at the home of one of the ladies just a few miles from the venue. As we ate and chatted, the telephone sounded.

Our hostess answered it in another part of the house. She was away for a lengthy period before returning with a dazed look on her face. The chatter in the room died down as all eyes fixed on her.

'That was Julie on the phone,' we were told quietly. Knowing the seriousness of her condition, everyone held their breath. Things could be bad.

'She's been to her doctor this morning. It seems she got to the waiting room at about a quarter before twelve for a mid-day consultation and waited to be called. At four minutes to twelve the secretary went into the waiting room and called her in. She told me, "As I stood to go into the consulting room, I felt something go through my body and I knew I was healed. When the doctor examined me, he said, 'I don't know why you're here. There is nothing wrong with you. I'm going to discharge you.' Jesus healed me, you know, Jesus healed me just before midday!" '

The time was precise, and the doctor had been on hand to check it out. You may imagine the effect this had on those in the room, where there was much rejoicing at the news.

Healing at a distance – is this a feasible matter, or was it just a co-incidence? It was Galileo Galilei who made the point that a phenomenon must be repeatable to be acceptable in a scientific environment, and I think that the same principle holds when we discuss spiritual issues.

A few years ago a claim was made by two researchers that they had developed a means to create cold nuclear fission – and on a small scale, having used what was virtually a kitchen table to support their experiment. The impact on the scientific community at large, and the power generating industry in particular, was huge. Here was the prospect of almost limitless power at very low cost. However, several attempts to reproduce the experiment failed, and the idea was quietly dropped.

More recently Einstein's work on relativity has been challenged with the publication of a report recording the tracking of sub-atomic particles known as neutrinos at the CERN laboratory in Switzerland. The neutrino speed was measured to exceed the speed of light, in that the journey time between the laboratory and the Grand Sasso laboratory in Italy 450 miles away was measured at 60 billionths of a second faster than light. If it had been confirmed, this observation would have negated Einstein's Special Theory of Relativity. The implications would have been huge, challenging eventually the foundations of physics. At first, repeating the experiment seemed to confirm the result; but, in checking the instrumentation, it was found that a loose connection in the circuitry accounted for the anomaly. When this was corrected, the result could not be repeated. Therefore the initial observation was held to be invalid.

Just as in scientific experience, so too in the world of Christian experience: it is as well to discover that there is a principle being followed and whether there is a precedent. For this we look to the Bible. That is why it is a lamp for our feet and a light for our path (see Psalm 119:105). Further, I can be assured that there is no valid experience in my Christian life that I cannot corroborate from Scripture. In the event that something comes up for discussion, the point of reference is the Bible. Quarrelling with Einstein's ideas on relativity only resulted in embarrassment on this occasion; quarrelling with the Bible will be worse.

In the matter of 'remote' healing, records exist of Jesus healing while the supplicant is absent, so there is good scriptural authority for it. Even so, are we right to anticipate such reports in the twenty-first century?

We are, even if they come in the most unexpected ways.

On another occasion, while I was speaking at a series of meetings on Jersey, the Lord gave me a word for a person with a complicated medical disorder. There was no response from anyone in the audience, but I prayed for the person nevertheless. After the meeting I was approached by a lady who wanted to tell me that what I had said exactly conformed to a medical condition her daughter had. The problem, however, was that her daughter lived in *New* Jersey in the USA, so there was no chance of her receiving the required ministry.

Or was there?

The next day I was approached by the same lady, this time in a state of high excitement. She had telephoned her daughter in New Jersey to relate the incident, when her daughter excitedly told her mother that a few hours before Jesus had healed her.

So far as we could judge, this was at the time we were praying for her on Jersey.

# 17.

# Hungry for the Lord

Over the years, parts of Canada became familiar territory to me, particularly Highway 401 which runs between Toronto in the west along Lake Ontario to Belleville and then on to Kingston, Ontario. This became a frequently travelled road since it took me to visit both my student at the Royal Military College at Kingston and the First Convention Baptist church of Belleville.

My first exposure to Belleville was to a Baptist denomination of which I had never heard (there are a lot of Baptist denominations in North America). The church building was large and airy. The great and the good turned up and filled the stage, while the congregation, many of whom were visitors, filled the rest of the building. A seat was reserved for me somewhere towards the middle of the assembly on stage. I knew no one there.

One of the organizers stood to welcome everyone and then proceeded to explain that the meeting had been organized by my friends; the elders wanted us to know that they had merely allowed their property to be hired for the occasion and they did not have any control over what might happen here. 'So I must repeat,' he persisted, 'these are not Baptist church meetings. If, therefore, this series of meetings is a total disaster, please don't blame the Baptists.'

I felt really welcomed!

And faith moved to a new level.

The week progressed and, evening by evening, the size of the congregation grew. My daily encounter with the pastor of the church became progressively more cordial and, as the end of the week approached, I learned that the meetings were to be extended to the Sunday, replacing the scheduled services in the morning and evening, finishing with a special barbeque.

Sunday morning arrived, and so did an unexpected congregation. About fifteen minutes before the service was scheduled to begin, as the pastor was informing me I had a maximum speaking time of ten minutes, we were interrupted by a knock on the vestry door. One of the elders looked in to say that there were rather more people present than usual. The pastor decided that I could be released on his flock for, maybe, fifteen minutes . . . could I manage that? In just a few minutes more, the same elder looked around the door to say that all the seats in the building were now full and there was a queue of people to get in and he would put out chairs in the aisles. My fifteen-minute limit was further extended to twenty. Again the elder appeared, now looking as if he was out of control of life: all the movable seats were now taken and people were sitting on the floors throughout all of the aisles in the sanctuary. At this point, the pastor metaphorically tore up his sheet of arrangements for the morning, looked at me in terror and said, 'Preach for as long as you like.'

That evening I was at the barbeque when the pastor decided that he would address his congregation. He told his folk how, as a young man, he had loved the Lord and wanted to serve Jesus. In due course he went to a theological college where all of his simple faith was educated out of him. He learned to question the deity of Christ, to destroy the virgin birth as a concept, and to discredit the miracles of Jesus. As a result he was ordained with nothing worth sharing.

He then went on to say that, at the beginning of this week, he had resented what I was preaching. But as the week advanced all the thoughts he had had as a young man were being revived. His hunger for a relationship with Jesus Christ had returned as he had been reminded of the things he had learned and experienced in his early Christian life. 'And now,' he added, 'I am dedicating myself again to the Lord. I am making a promise to this congregation that I will, in future, only preach from the Bible.'

There was further spin-off from that week. A couple of evenings later I went with my hosts to dinner in a local restaurant. They brought with them a couple of friends who wanted to talk about the previous week, as they had heard rumours. The friends had brought their son and daughter-in-law for support. Questions flowed: what was the work of the Holy Spirit; how do people meet God; what part does Jesus play; how do people get healed; what is speaking in tongues?

Then things got a little more pointed. What about us? Have we been filled with the Holy Spirit? Could we be? When? Now? Then where?

Trying to look as if this is what I did daily before breakfast, I suggested that we should retire to one of the cars in the car park outside. So the older couple and I sat in the back seat of their enormous vehicle, and we prayed, and the Lord visited us with his Holy Spirit. In moments both husband and wife were laid out in the enormous foot-well of the car. The couple became quite excited as, in praising God, they found themselves speaking in tongues in a most uninhibited manner.

What I was doing, as a thermodynamicist, I really couldn't establish, but everything happening before me ticked a box in my understanding of the Bible. That took primacy over my fundamental building blocks of thinking, those two laws of thermodynamics.

Eventually they calmed down, the car stopped shaking and peace returned. We went back into the restaurant to find every eye in this rather elegant establishment watching us closely. Our friends' children immediately demanded to know what had been happening. A half-whispered discussion then led to the two adult children turning to me and asking, 'And what about us?'

A few minutes later the three of us retired to the car park, everyone in the restaurant by now having abandoned their food to observe the proceedings in silence.

In the sanctuary of the car we prayed again. The Holy Spirit rewarded their hungry hearts, the car shook as they were baptized in the Holy Spirit, the two recipients said something along the lines of 'Wow' and we returned to the restaurant.

There was no movement of waiters, no clatter of cutlery or crockery, no chatter. Every person present watched in silence as we returned to our seats, the young couple grinning uncontrollably as the parents had done before them. We sat in silence for several moments until I leant forward to say quietly to my host, 'Why is everybody in this place watching us? Have we disturbed them?'

'Simple – they all think that you're shooting dope!'

Later I had a speaking commitment well up into the north. It seemed as if we drove for ever into the gloom of a Canadian evening in the Northern Territories, to arrive at a Dutch Reformed church which appeared to be set nowhere, so I was agreeably surprised to find that we were not the only ones present: a lengthy queue stretched out of the building and into the darkness.

To say that these people were hungry for the Lord would be a massive understatement. I spoke for about an hour but was urged on and on – and on. From memory I would say that I spoke for about two and a half hours, and I lost count of the number of those who prayed to meet Jesus Christ.

This was all new to the congregation but it seemed that the Lord had not finished yet. Earlier on, when I had been standing in the queue waiting my turn to get into the building, I had noticed a young woman ahead of me. I became convinced that she had a particular medical condition and that the Lord was going to heal her that evening.

During the time that I was speaking the moment came to share this piece of news. Pointing at the young lady, I asked her if she had a medical condition which I then described. To my joy she confirmed that was the case. We prayed right then and immediately the girl was able to declare her healing.

Suddenly it was clear that the discomfort of travelling through a northern Canadian night, very cold and remarkably uncomfortable, was worth it. A couple of hundred people, all of whom knew each other in that sparsely populated area, saw something of the reality of Jesus Christ that they had never perceived before. If anything excites me more than I can describe, it is to be in a group of people who are seeing for the first time some new aspect of Jesus.

That's life-changing – their paradigm shift.

The opportunity to face up to the challenge of international ministry without the sort of support to which I was accustomed – in both my scientific domain and Christian circles – occurred early on in my walk with the Lord.

I had been invited to go to Ottawa to be the main speaker at a major breakfast meeting in downtown Ottawa. I had no scientific contacts in that region – in fact, I knew no one there at all. I'd been in something of a daze when I had accepted the invitation, but now the date approached I began to assess the enormity of the situation. The whole of my professional training had been along conservative lines: in the business of science you always worked out a back-up position in case things went wrong. But here there was no back-up position: I couldn't even slip off home since that was going to be about 3,500 miles away. I sat on the flight with a measure of terror: I was used to transatlantic crossings by now, but this was something different. At 35,000 feet I was wondering about the possibility of getting off!

Arriving in Ottawa, I had no idea who I would be meeting. It was with clear relief that I saw a man, expectant smile on his face, weaving his way through the crowd. Then he stood in front of me. 'Roy Peacock?' he asked.

I was relieved. 'How did you recognize me?' Perhaps this was to be a feature of the life of Christian ministry: the world could recognize the man of God in a crowd, drawn by the glow emanating from him. The explanation was somewhat more mundane: 'I saw your photograph on the cover of your recent book.'

I was taken to the hotel where the next morning's meeting was to be held. On the way there we went over the details for the next day. It seemed that the hotel was good but the booking numbers were disappointing. 'The problem is, we had a big draw last month when Michael Harper was speaking – he always attracts a crowd. We had twelve hundred people attend that breakfast. But this month I must apologize that the numbers are down.'

'How many?' (I was asking myself frantically, twenty, maybe thirty?)

'And we've laid up a lot of literature as well,' I was told. Not only was this morning going to be a crashing failure, it was going to be an expensive crashing failure.

'So how many are attending?' I asked, dreading to hear the answer yet feeling that I should share their pain.

'We've only got eight hundred booked in,' though he added hastily, 'Maybe some more will arrive without having booked.'

Did I even know what eight hundred people looked like?

But the question I put to him was, 'How do you get eight hundred fried eggs to be ready at the same time?'

His voice remained full of apologies: 'Will you mind this?'

'Not at all,' I responded hastily, and with my voice suitably sad, resigned but forgiving, I whispered, 'I'm sure I'll cope.'

Eight hundred people, I thought. Outside of Strasbourg I had never seen that many in a congregation before.

My hotel room was unlike anything I had encountered before. It was palatial. In fact it was so splendid I thought it would be wrong to waste my time sleeping in it. My hosts' money would be better spent if I sat up all night to admire the surroundings.

Once we had eaten breakfast the next morning, the proceedings began. I was assured we would be away well before lunchtime: 'We always are.' Eventually I was introduced, stood and looked over the sea of faces. All I could do was talk about Jesus, but that was all that was necessary. The atmosphere became electric and, at the conclusion, those who did not know Christ were invited to yield their lives and experience the new birth. The response was astonishing. My hosts guided me away at 2.30 p.m., while the counselling and individual prayer continued – all of the material, books, flyers and papers having been exhausted. I had known eight and a half hours of ministry! Exhausted, I walked on air.

Thermodynamics was fading into a secondary position in my thinking, but my thought processes were still the same: I was still checking everything I saw against my scientific understanding. But now I had just three categories of analysis: what God was doing was either miraculous or providential or simply in the Lord's supporting hand.

That first visit to Ottawa led to more, one of which included an invitation to speak at the Church of the Redeemer. It was warm weather so all of the doors of the building were wide open. After I had finished speaking, people were challenged to come forward. They did so and, in front of the congregation (not in a side room where they normally prayed for people) the Holy Spirit did his work.

Participation of the congregation was intense as they cried out to God. In fact the noise was so loud that one man, walking on the other side of the main road, heard the congregation through the open doors, crossed the road and stood in the doorway where he enquired what was going on. The doorman said he had no idea but referred him to me. He therefore walked into the congregation to speak to me, but was immediately overcome by the presence of God and fell down. Later, when he rose from the ground, it was found he had been born again and filled with the Holy Spirit.

Towards the end of another long itinerary in Canada I said in passing, 'I always know when I have been away from home long enough – it's when I've used up all my socks!'

The comment raised more than a laugh. The next evening meeting was my last before flying home. Towards the end I was approached by an elderly lady who had attended all of the meetings in that place. She pressed a neatly wrapped package into my hand, and then she fled.

Later on I opened the package to find a beautifully knitted pair of socks – my size, of course!

During the course of another series at the same church, my talk was interrupted by a woman standing in the congregation, halting the flow of the meeting and asking if she could say something. That was all right with me, and so she told of her sister who was grievously ill, and she requested that I pray for her. In response to several questions over the heads of the audience we learned that 'No' the sister was not a Christian and 'No' the lady was not prepared to talk to her sister about the Lord. So I responded by saying, 'I won't pray for your sister's healing, but I will pray, right now, that the Lord will work in your heart and give you the ability to speak to your sister – that you will lead her to the Lord and she will be born again.'

And that is how I prayed. As is so often the case, I expected no feedback.

Three years later I was flying from Heathrow to Strasbourg and using what turned out to be a very local airline whose route took passengers on a four-stop tour of Northern Europe to get to Strasbourg. The aircraft was an early turboprop whose seats were designed with a space between adjacent backs, allowing a passenger to see anyone immediately ahead. At the time of boarding, I couldn't help noticing three women in the queue since they were evidently enjoying the occasion very much and, being extroverts, were quite happy for all the other passengers to know about it. I groaned inwardly, hankering after a quiet life.

Things were not made better when I realized that two of the ladies were seated directly in front of me, while the third was forced to sit at the front of the aircraft.

As the engines revved up and the aircraft began to roll along the tarmac, it occurred to me that things had grown very quiet with the ladies just before me. Glancing through the gap in the back-rests in front, I could see that one of the women was white with fear, her hands gripping the armrests and a pronounced look of strain on her face.

We landed at the first of our intermediate stops, and the lady in front relaxed slightly as conversation was resumed. Feeling sorry for her, I leant forward to say that the aircraft was really quite safe, and that it made all of those noises as a matter of course and she could relax. Her friend, who had been watching her travelling companion closely, was evidently relieved. During the flight so far the friend had opened her passport and read it closely, there being little else to divert attention. The passport was of Canadian issue and I could see that the owner's name was Barbara Oswald.

As we waited for the flight to continue, I asked Mrs Oswald where she came from in Canada. She looked at me in surprise and blurted out, 'Gee, how do you know I'm Canadian? On this side of the Atlantic, most people mistake me for an American.'

'It's amazing what people know, Mrs Oswald – Barbara.' Noticing the very large Bible on her knee, I added to embellish the joke: 'And I expect that you are on your way to the Christian convention in Strasbourg.' Mrs Oswald's eyes opened wide and her mouth dropped open; it was then that I realized this joke with a stranger was taking on a life of its own.

'He knows my name,' Barbara blurted out to her friend, who was now more interested in what was happening in front of her than in the immediate prospect of crashing in flames. 'He knows my name.' She said it again and again.

Down the length of the aircraft cabin, Barbara shouted, 'Janie! Hey, Janie!' Janie turned. And at the top of her voice Barbara announced to Janie – and to all in between – 'Janie, you'd better come back here. We've got a prophet in the seat behind us.'

As one, the whole passenger complement froze. Silence descended as, with almost military precision, everyone turned to look at the prophet just behind Barbara. At this point I was starting to hope that the aircraft might obligingly crash in flames to deliver me from the embarrassment of a joke gone wild.

Things calmed down somewhat and I asked Barbara once more where she came from. 'Ottawa.' I said that I knew it. As we talked further Barbara looked closely at me and, her eyes narrowing, she said, 'I know you. I've heard you speak in Ottawa. Your name is . . . your name is . . . Peacock. You are Bob Peacock.'

'Roy Peacock, actually.'

'Yes, that's right,' she confirmed my name, 'Roy Peacock. I heard you speak in the Church of the Redeemer one night. In fact, I interrupted you as you were speaking to ask if you would pray for my sister who was very ill.' Memories came flooding back and I was able to repeat to her what I had said on that earlier occasion.

By way of confirmation, she added, 'You said that you would not pray for my sister's healing but that she would be saved and that I would lead her to the Lord.' (In fact, those were not my precise words, as I had said that I would pray for her to have the ability to lead her sister to the Lord.) 'Now, let me tell you what happened. I got home. I'd always been fearful of talking about spiritual things, but I went to see my sister who was in bed. I began talking about Jesus and found that she was hungry to know! We prayed together and my sister was converted right there.

'The change in her life was astonishing. After that she

talked to everyone about Jesus. She led every member of the family to the Lord – my mother, my husband, the children. Over a two-year period every member of our family was converted. Then, just a year ago, her illness was taking its toll and she became very weak. My mother and I visited her and we sat, one on either side of her bed. There was little to say but, at one point, my sister looked at me and then at our mother. "Mummy," she said, "I am very tired. I'd really like to go and be with Jesus. May I?"

'My mother's heart was heavy – she had no desire for her to go anywhere. But she said, "Yes, if that's what you want."

'Turning to me, my sister said, "I would really like to go to be with Jesus. Can I go?"

'"Yes, you can go."

'My mother and I each held one of her hands and we, all three of us, prayed together. We said amen and sat for a moment in silence. When we opened our eyes to look at her, she had gone.'

# 18.

# A Taste of Heaven

Anybody reading these chapters could be excused for concluding that this is a manifesto for triumphalism, where every incident, issue or crisis is met by the introduction of the Lord Jesus at a critical moment, and the miracles flow seamlessly one after the other, victorious moment upon victorious moment. But it hasn't been quite like that.

I have known good health over most of my life and, when I've been ill (my blindness being a case in point) I have been able to report a good and speedy outcome. That was until a little while ago, when everything imaginable seemed to happen. Pains in my left leg became progressively worse, resulting in some manipulation of my spine which in turn led to a scan which revealed it had effectively collapsed. The discs in the lower back were squeezed very thin, and the vertebrae were in consequence worn in a non-symmetrical manner – a random stack of bones. This was put down to the result of a misspent youth playing too much rugby and squash. My osteopath found it unbelievable that I had no back pain.

At the same time an irregularity was detected in my heart-beat, and this led to a variety of tests. As I write this

I continue to wear a monitor inserted in my chest while cardiac specialists are still trying to work out what is going on. The heart problem seems to have initiated another difficulty. Walking my dogs one morning I was climbing the last hill in returning to my car when I became, quite unexpectedly, totally exhausted and could find nowhere to rest. Realizing that my breadth of vision was rapidly narrowing, I knew that I was going to faint. And then I tumbled over. Unconscious before I hit the rough stone pathway, I made contact with the ground face-first, my hands by my side not having done their job.

I don't know how long I was unconscious, but I regained consciousness to have a ground level view of the road down which, about a hundred yards away, a car had stopped. A couple had jumped out and were running up the road towards me. I was aware that my two dogs had sat themselves down, one on either side of me, to guard me and, as my rescuers ran towards me, the younger dog let out a low and menacing growl – which continued until I told her to shut up. Raising my head, I saw a pool of blood on the ground and detected a stream of blood pouring from my head into the pool. It was then that I knew something was seriously wrong. I was quickly taken to the local hospital to get cleaned up, examined and stuck back together.

Having dealt with the obvious things, the doctor in the local hospital turned her attention to my nose: it was bent sideways. The doctor instructed me to look directly at her, caught hold of my nose and bent it straight with a firm jerk . . . one of the more painful experiences of my life. Now I was in agony with my nose – and not a pretty sight!

As time advanced, so my medical condition became more extreme. Spinal specialists and cardiac specialists all wanted to get things done.

Our home is a predominantly single-storey structure, but it is also very long and narrow. In my reduced physical circumstances it could now take me up to seven minutes to get from one end to the other. With matters getting worse I was standing, one morning, in the bathroom, hanging on to a low wall which is really an architectural feature and trying to turn around. The pain was quite excruciating. I paused while making the turn, hoping that the waves of pain would subside.

Suddenly everything changed. I was no longer in my home but was transported. I was walking in a large expanse of brilliantly white clouds at my feet and the bluest sky over my head. The whole atmosphere was clean and pure beyond measure. In my heart I knew joy unspeakable as I walked in this astonishing environment.

This was heaven.

Over the years I have been a Christian I had, like anyone, sought to know something about heaven. I had read about it, talked about it, listened to sermons on it. But, quite frankly, nothing seemed to have an authentic ring; it was more a discussion about possibilities rather than the account of someone who had been there and now brought back the experience to thrill me.

Yet now I stood in heaven; I walked in heaven.

I had been transported from my bathroom to a different location, one with which I was not familiar. I stood in the open air, looking across a landscape to a horizon, unimpeded in every direction. The sky above me was cloudless and an intense clear blue. The ground on which I stood was obscured by a layer of thick white cloud, and I walked without being hampered in any way. I really was in heaven, in an atmosphere that was warm and vibrant.

The whole atmosphere was clean and pure beyond measure. I was walking with God, even though I couldn't see him. In front of me, and a little to my left, a figure appeared, walking over the horizon and advancing purposefully in my direction. This person was dressed in a full length white robe. He had his arms extended as if to welcome me, and the look on his face was unforgettable: it was radiant. Over his head, with a depth of about eight inches, there was a layer of something that, while fully transparent, included myriads of golden stars in its make-up. The stars were glittering and, together with the transparent layer, made what appeared to be a veil draped from shoulder to shoulder and over the head. As I focused on this figure, it was with amazement that I recognized him: it was me.

I felt an overwhelming flow of love such as I have never previously known, flowing through me and from me. Standing as an observer, outside of myself, I watched as I lifted my arms wide as in a greeting, and the flow of love became indescribable. Then, as I continued to watch, I followed the eyes of my alter-ego, and looked to my right to see what the object of such joy might be. There I saw Elizabeth, walking quite purposely towards me. She too was dressed in a white gown, her head also surrounded by a cloud of shimmering gold. My alter-ego embraced her. I realized afresh my love for Elizabeth, yet at a more intense level than I had ever known. It was the moment of a lifetime. It was life-changing.

There was a lengthy silence as I hung on to her. Then I spoke: 'It's all right now.' She was no longer alone; in fact a fear of loneliness had been banished from her life. She would never be alone again.

After a long pause, I added in clear definitive terms, 'It's all over,' and I knew it was. There had been a cost in dedicating our lives to Jesus Christ. We had lost friends. I had lost professional opportunities. Our children had missed many of the things that growing families might do, the family holidays we might have had in different circumstances – just for being Christians. But I knew that those were matters that had been dealt with and could trouble us no further. Nobody could hurt us any more.

Finally, hugging her, I said, 'We are free,' and I knew that this was so. We were free of the chains of the world, free of enemies, free of the people who had attacked us for political, denominational or personal reasons, free to be the people that the Lord had prepared us to be. And eternity waited before us. This was a moment I wanted never to end, surrounded by heaven and having Elizabeth held securely in my arms.

Then everything changed. I was back in the bathroom, clinging to the wall to support myself and avoid falling over, as I tried to turn towards the doorway.

Reflecting on this, I realized that the things we had endured in our Christian lives, the rejection of friends, of people and churches, the moments of need, the disappointment and despair, meant nothing at all. Writing to the Corinthians,

Paul referred to love that endures all things (see 1 Corinthians 13:7). Of Jesus, our exemplar, the writer to the Hebrews says that Jesus 'for the joy that was set before him endured . . .' (Hebrews 12:2). For Jesus, it was to endure the cross. Paul knew something of that experience, 'cast down, but not destroyed' (2 Corinthians 4:9). And maybe, for me, there has been a measure of what James calls the 'trying' or testing of our faith (see James 1:3).

But this one thing I know: I have had a glimpse of the joy that is set before me. I could not eradicate this from my memory, even if I wanted to. These were moments in heaven. I have walked with my God, Jesus. I have heard Jesus. From that time the past meant nothing to me. I could put behind me all that had gone before and now, with certainty, I could 'press toward the mark for the prize of the high calling of God in Christ Jesus' (Philippians 3:14).

When, later on, I described this experience to Elizabeth, she had a question for me: 'Were my wrinkles gone?'

'You had no wrinkles and you didn't limp,' I answered. 'Your hair was dark.'

Jesus had done a good work.

> . . . now we are children of God; and it has not yet been revealed what we shall be, but we know that when He is revealed, we shall be like Him, for we shall see Him as He is.
>
> 1 John 3:2-3 [NKJV]

# Postscript

It began as a word spoken, as it seemed, out of nowhere, and that word was an almost unknown piece of ancient writing: 'The harvest is passed, the summer is ended and we are not saved.' In the middle of a sleepless night, this struck fear into me and started a wrestling with the God I did not know. By the morning I was determined to banish from my mind the challenging and frightening events of the previous night. That determination, plus a day's work on the vintage car of the moment, brought little relief, especially as my wife now declared that she had met God. She encouraged me – or perhaps I should say ordered me – to go to that final gospel meeting of the week.

I went to the service, was deeply challenged by the sermon of a man I had grown quickly to despise over the week, and was spurred on by a knowledge that something fundamental was missing in my life – something that had now been discovered by Elizabeth. So, taking myself in hand, I made a decision. (Did I make it, or was it being presented to me in a manner that forbade refusal?) I had determined that if I was to commit my life to God, then this essentially personal matter would remain so – no one in this life would ever know that I, an upwardly mobile research student in one of the world's leading centres of philosophical expression and scientific advancement, had made this commitment. But I was quickly to discover that I couldn't keep this promise. From the moment that I made the commitment – through a simple act of taking a red book in my hand – I have wanted anyone who will listen to know about the Jesus I have met.

This memoir is inevitably a much abridged version of what has happened in consequence so far. It has been an experience eclipsing my fulfilling research in the fields of fluid mechanics and aeronautics. Yes, it still gives me pleasure to board an aircraft, to look into the intake and, on occasions, see the turbo-machinery idling over and to be able to say to myself, 'I did that.' Yet to meet someone, somewhere in the world, whose life has been changed by Jesus Christ, and to be there to see it happen, has no parallel.

In terms of experience, these two lifestyles were of opposite polarity – yet I was discovering that they could co-exist. Any first-year physics student will tell you that opposite magnetic poles are mutually attractive. So perhaps it should not be surprising that a rationalistic scientist might find the mystery, the demonstration and the results of the Christian life to be attractive.

The ministry that followed my paradigm shift began with five unconverted people meeting in our home, guided by David as we explored the Bible – never, it seems, getting beyond John, Chapter 1, verse 1. And just as that was an effortless exercise outside of our earnest prayers, so too was everything that has followed. This memoir has traced that progress – not in an exhaustive way, but like a pebble skimming over a pond, touching down from time to time to record a disturbance in the water. Without any solicitation whatsoever on my part, I have spoken on every continent to congregations as small as a dozen and as large as several thousands.

We lost count years ago of the numbers who have committed their lives to Jesus, his compassion for them so clear; and of those who have been prepared for service as they have been filled with the Holy Spirit; and of the many whose bodies have been healed, as deaf ears and blind eyes have been opened, legs restored to their correct length, and a wide variety of afflictions dealt with by the Saviour who hasn't changed one little bit from Bible days.

My elder son was challenged in conversation one day by an unbeliever saying that the Christian claims were beyond reason and belief. He replied: 'When you've seen the things that I saw as a child, you could never doubt the reality of Jesus Christ.'

The house in which we lived in Bedfordshire had a fine garden, stretching down a slight hill to its boundary, with an acre or so of grass. The garden was sub-divided into three: a formal and pretty ancient upper garden, surrounded by very ancient walls; a main area, a slope consisting entirely of grass (because that represented the limit of my creative ability) bounded at its lower side by a dense and tall hedge; and then, at the end of a short tunnel, an ecological garden, as I liked to call it, though everyone else could see it was a rubbish tip. It was this third part of the garden which formed the focus of a strange, vivid and unforgettable dream.

A visitor, a Christian woman, had shown eagerness to look at our gardens, and I was walking her around the upper garden. We looked at the rather straggly roses and what passed as a herbaceous border, including a rare and particularly ugly species of daisy. We moved on to the middle garden and, as we passed the dense and tall hedge, our visitor noticed the tunnel. In the dream the tunnel was covered by a crushed velvet curtain, completely obscuring any view beyond.

'What is through there, Roy?' she asked.

'That's a private garden.'

'May I go through, please?'

'No, I'm sorry. That's not possible. That garden is solely for Elizabeth and me. No one else ever goes there.'

'Why is that? I would really like to look inside.'

'No. You see, that is the garden of our tears. It's not for public gaze. No one is allowed to see the private sorrows we have known. There's a part of our lives that must remain our own.'

'But, Roy – please let me just take a quick look.' To my despair she prevailed, and so I drew back the crushed velvet curtain. She didn't try to go into the area but simply looked through at what I knew to be the rubbish tip. But the view was changed – and now it was breathtaking. From one end to the other this part of the garden was filled with bright, multi-coloured flowers. The sun was shining out of a clear blue sky, while butterflies and small birds busied themselves around everything, from small pansies to tall hollyhocks. For a moment the woman was speechless. Then, turning towards me, she said with gravity,

'When you share the story of this garden, Roy, the world will be blessed.'

In this memoir we have lifted the crushed velvet curtain just a little, and you have peeped over our shoulders.

There is a 'pearl of great price' and it's worth every penny (Matthew 13:45-46).

And it can be yours.

# Appendix

# The Laws of Thermodynamics

Over much of the first half of the nineteenth century a number of scientists attempted to understand thermodynamics – James Joule, Sadi Carnot and Lord Kelvin among those at the forefront. The driving force was the Franco-British rivalry that had already spilled over into the battlefield (and still does on the rugby field). The French couldn't understand the reasons for British superiority in war until this was eventually ascribed to the role of the steam engine in British military production.

There's nothing for focusing the mind like a good war, and this was no different. Efforts to understand the nature of heat and energy were made the more difficult as various researchers attempted to discover a *single* law that described the behaviour of energy. Carnot tried to define energy by a commodity he called caloric, but his ideas didn't work. Joules made progress in his workshop in a corner of his father's brewery. His experiment used what has become known as a Joules paddle, essential for any student in a laboratory doing experiments with heat. (It is said that thermodynamicists have used beer liberally ever since for all sorts of applications, not least drowning their sorrows when experiments and bright ideas don't go to plan.)

It remained for Sir William Thompson (a.k.a. Lord Kelvin) to unlock the mystery. He proposed that any process was governed not by one but by *two* independent laws, and that these laws operated within a system constrained only by a flexible, impermeable surface. (To get the picture, think of a children's balloon inflated in the usual manner.) These became known as the Two Laws of Thermodynamics, independent relationships describing first the *indestructibility* of energy and second its *unavailability*.

These two laws, according to Kelvin, were central to any process in the universe, and this has never yet been disproved. Whether a person is a thermodynamicist, a chemist, a biologist, or an engineer is irrelevant: the two laws are there, in your face or lurking in the background, establishing the immutability of the scientific process – from cosmology to biology.

## The First Law

The First Law of Thermodynamics is not difficult to understand. It tells us that energy cannot be created or destroyed, but it can change its shape.

By way of illustration, let us consider a kilo of water. If frozen, this becomes a kilo of ice and then, if boiled, becomes the same weight in steam. This principle of conservation is similar to what happens to energy within a system. Replacing the kilo of water by, say, a gallon of petrol for use in a car engine, we find the following. The petrol has a total energy level which is locked up in the chemical composition of the fuel. The fuel is burned in the engine cylinder when the energy is released. Part of that energy is transformed into the power that drives the wheels, making the car move. Another part of the energy heats up the exhaust gas which then goes to the atmosphere, warming that up a little. A further part of the energy coming from the fuel is absorbed as friction in the engine and this is routed to the atmosphere through the car's radiator and any heat exchangers that may be present. Finally, aerodynamic drag – wind resistance – is overcome using energy which then also warms up the atmosphere. To all of these uses of energy we can add the occasional use of the brakes. When all of these component energies are added up, the result is that the total energy used is equal to the total energy initially in the gallon of fuel.

This is the First Law in action. It demonstrates in simple, physical form what the first Law is stating in more general terms: that whatever shape it assumes, the quantity of heat or energy (these are the same thing) remains constant. So we conclude that, irrespective of the form that the energy or heat is in (and there are numerous forms available), the total amount is always constant in a system.

## The Second Law

The Second Law is less intuitively obvious. This law uses a parameter called entropy, itself a relatively difficult concept. Entropy is an evaluation of what we may call the unavailability of energy. The Second Law indicates that entropy is increased in any real process, no matter what we may have expected in theory.

Scientists are often divided into two types – natural scientists and applied scientists. It is said that the applied scientists do it for money and the natural scientists, being made of superior stuff, do not dirty their hands with such things. It goes (perhaps without saying) that the natural scientists comprise a species apart – although actually the same rules, equations and methodology are used by each. I make this point because it puts into context a remark published by a well-known Cambridge professor in one branch of the natural sciences in an article he was writing:

> The trouble with Peacock is that he is an engineer. He is rather like the village boot-maker who had just made a pair of shoes for one of his children and could speak of nothing else. Peacock's problem is that he can speak of nothing other than the second law of Thermodynamics as if everything depended on that.

Thus charged in a court of law, I would have to say, 'Guilty, m' Lud!' since all science eventually hinges on these two laws.

Sir Arthur Eddington, born in 1882, became the Plumian Professor of Astronomy and Experimental Philosophy in 1914, and was also Director of the Cambridge University Observatories. He was known as an able communicator in clear language, making profound contributions to science, especially in validating Einstein's General Theory of Relativity. Eddington was not a man with whom to cross swords. Of the Second Law he said this:

The law that entropy always increases – the Second Law of Thermodynamics – holds, I think, the supreme position among the laws of nature. If someone points out to you that your pet theory of the Universe is in disagreement with Maxwell's equations – then so much the worse for Maxwell's equations. If it is found to be contradicted by observation – well, these experimentalists do bungle things sometimes. But if your theory is found to be against the Second Law of Thermodynamics I can give you no hope: there is nothing left for it but to collapse in deepest humiliation.[1]

Let's take a look at what is involved here and the background. It was in the early nineteenth century that the industrial revolution began. For this great work to be done some means of powering the production processes had to be devised – and the steam engine, in its earliest and most primitive form, was seen as the means.

That the steam engine worked was clear, but how did it work? That was when Lord Kelvin made his great contribution, and the two Laws were established. Since then it has been found that any and every process in the universe is governed by these two laws – something which, while conceptually breathtaking, we ignore regularly.

The implications of this are profound. It introduces the concept of aging and decay. If you have difficulty in recognizing that the Second Law is doing its work, then join me by looking in the mirror every morning. When I look I see the haggard lines on my face, the greying hair, the silver stubble on my chin and the general aspect of the world-weary. And I note that the Second Law is alive and well – even if I am not!

Now, I make these points to emphasize this – whether you are looking down a telescope or into a microscope – the two laws are always being obeyed. The only times they are not go by the name of 'miracles'. It is for this reason that, within the scientific orbit, miracles are not accounted for; or it is said that they 'do not exist'.

Nevertheless, as I have sought to show in this book, the fact that they do exist can be identified in scientific terms. This provides us with a definition of a miracle as an event in which:

1. the First Law of Thermodynamics is being violated, or
2. the Second Law of Thermodynamics is being violated, or
3. both Laws of Thermodynamics are being violated, or
4. the laws of Thermodynamics are being obeyed but at a rate that is not statistically normal.

Let me give you some examples.

**First Law violation**

Some people have two legs which are not equal in length. This may be congenital, or the result of an accident in life. The person finds walking difficult and asks for prayer. Ensuring that the legs are not twisted in any way, nor subject to twisting, the candidate is prayed for and one leg is carefully observed to grow. (The maximum growth I have ever observed is about four-and-a-half inches.) Such a miracle is a First Law violation.

The first occasion that I saw a leg grow was at a meeting in our home in Bedfordshire. I was so excited I exclaimed to a colleague, 'Just wait until we get to the men's meeting on Friday. This will amaze them when I tell them what I've seen.'

'Don't bother,' he replied rather drily. 'They will never believe you.' And, sadly, he was right. That did not alter the fact that I had witnessed a miracle. The person healed was the wife of a senior scientist working for the government. Watching her later that evening walking up the road to her car, I noticed that she was unable to direct herself in a straight line but walked in a series of arcs with corrections to point herself in the right direction. She had yet to learn to accommodate the different stride of each leg. This was simply further confirmation of what the Lord had done.

## Second Law violation

I was speaking recently in a parish church in Oxfordshire, where a lady responded to the invitation to receive prayer. She recorded that for twenty years she had had an ongoing neck problem. Twenty years before this particular evening she had been hit in the side of the head by a baseball which had jarred her neck. In consequence, whenever she turned her head she could feel the neck joints grinding or sometimes clicking. After prayer the noises reduced, such that there was only a slight clicking. Following further prayer, the neck joint operated smoothly and without any clicks or grinds.

Bones and joints don't normally become less worn. We can say that this was a violation of the Second Law.

## A statistically improbable change of rate

Some years ago, during a normal day's work in the academic business, I realized that I was late for the beginning of a lecture I was due to give. While running towards the Lecture Theatre I dived into the men's room, not noticing that the floor had been recently washed. I slipped badly, falling and skidding under the door of one of the cubicles.

Some time later I was found unconscious by a colleague who saw my feet sticking out from beneath the door. Considering that to be a little unusual, he hauled me out by my feet, my head jamming between the wall and the lavatory plinth, thus probably doing more damage than the original fall. As consciousness returned, I rushed into my lecture and delivered it in extreme pain before going home to lie down. My sight was obscured by a bag of blood hanging just above one eye, and the pain was quite unbearable.

The next day in the department was a source of humour for those who learned that I had been found with my feet sticking out of the lavatory stall. The Head of the Department heard of this and took a more serious view of what had happened: he ordered me to the Institute doctor immediately. I was transferred to the local hospital for X-rays, a somewhat worrying process as the radiologist kept on asking me back into the inspection room to take further shots.

I was discharged in time to go for the weekend to Exmouth for a preparation meeting involving the team of a very large summer camp. My pain continued, tending to become a dull but pervading ache, when it transpired that a speaker at one session asked people to go forward for prayer. With what I now believed to be a cracked skull I stood at the front until Michael came to me. Instead of asking me what I had come to the front for, he simply prayed for me, for the ministry God had given us, for my family, for my children – in fact he prayed for everything about me except my head! I wanted to stop him and point to my head, but he was in full flow. He said amen and moved on.

As I returned to my seat I realized that something odd was happening in my head. It felt like a sharp needle being pressed into me at the vital spot where the pain was at a maximum; but this needle was icy cold as it touched my skull, inside the eye socket. The feeling moved slowly across my head, from the eye socket out to the brow of my forehead and then across to the top of my cranium, where it stopped – after which I realized that the pain had gone.

Immediately after the meeting I sought out a medical student I knew was on the team.

'I have a question for you. Tell me, when a fractured bone heals, is the process endothermic or exothermic?' She looked at me oddly, thought it out and said,

'If a fracture is being healed, new material is being created to seal the crack. If new material is being created then heat is being absorbed in the process, so it is an endothermic process. Why do you ask?'

I explained what seemed to have been happening and she agreed that if the healing process had been accelerated then the temperature difference could conceivably be felt. 'But, of course,' she added, 'the blood circulation will wash the temperature difference out.'

'But if this happened in a couple of minutes rather than months, the temperature difference might not have time to be washed out.'

On that we agreed, and I was able to conclude that, while the mechanics of what I believed was happening to my skull was exactly as normal, the rate at which it happened was quite abnormal. A miracle.

This point about probability is important. Aficionados of the Second Law may say, 'The two laws of Thermodynamics hold within a closed system.' We have already noted that a system can be described as a volume whose boundary is impervious yet flexible, rather like a balloon but one across whose surface nothing can transfer – including entropy. It is claimed that the entropy generated in the system we have been examining must have migrated to a remote corner of the limiting envelope.

But entropy is not a commodity that one can carry in a bucket to a different location; it is a condition, so the argument is unlikely if not impossible.

Consider an experiment to illustrate. I place before me two flasks, each approximately half full of identical liquid, other than that one is in a low-entropy condition and the other in a high-entropy condition. Also one contains red dye while the other is clear. I pour the contents of one flask into the other. Rapidly they mix so that the resulting liquid is now pale red. The two liquids are now fully mixed, the properties of each being shared with the other to create a uniform mixture. Just as the red dye has mixed so have other properties, including the entropy, and they are uniform throughout. That's the way of things. I do not anticipate the red dye to migrate to one corner of the flask, nor do I anticipate that any of the properties of each liquid will remain isolated.

Scientific thinking does not say that a preferential migration of the red dye to a corner of the flask cannot take place: it can, but the *statistical probability* of that happening is so small that it doesn't. In the general process of decay – of entropy increase – in the universe, the same principles hold true. In fact, the picture drawn by many cosmologists of the end of the universe is a condition known as the heat death. At this point, all the thermodynamic processes involving heat and energy in the universe will have been completed, and a uniform thermodynamic picture results.

For many, such quantifying is an unnecessary detail, but irrespective of whether I am working in a scientific context or a spiritual environment, the mechanism is unchanged. As a result I am able to identify in sharper detail what God is doing, and to him goes the glory.

---

[1]   Sir Arthur Stanley Eddington, *The Nature of the Physical World* (New York: Cambridge University Press, 1928), p. 74.

# Acknowledgements

Without the dedicated input into our lives of David Laycock there would have been no story to report. It was he who challenged us initially, led Elizabeth to the Lord, and then made himself available at any time to bring support, advice and direction. The Revd Harry Sutton, then Secretary of the South American Missionary Society, preached in my local church, bringing me into a conviction that sealed matters – and I was born again.

Over the early years of our Christian lives there were several ministers whose effect on us was profound. The late Revd Dr Richard P Carter of Atlanta, Georgia, became a close personal friend and provided the jaw-dropping experience of his ministry where we saw what I can only describe as a prophet of God. It was shortly afterwards that we met the Revd Dr Ernest Soady of Los Angeles, California, now a life-long friend, who also demonstrated in his remarkable ministry those attributes of the Holy Spirit's presence for which all Christians should hunger. The Revd Jean Darnall, who also became a personal friend, taught us by her example the attributes of Christian ministry. The late John Hutchison, originally of the Parachute Regiment and hotelier, further demonstrated to us the validity of the work of the Holy Spirit in Christian ministry. The late John Hamilton, 'half-pint Hammie', was at all times one of those great encouragers, faithful in his preaching and in demonstrating the gifts of the Holy Spirit.

Over many years we were fortunate to know the support of the Trustees of the Carpenters Trust, John Elphinston, Michael Fenton-Jones, Alan Bell, Michael Carter and the late John Kerr.

In the scientific field, two people among many giants stand out, the late Jim Yost, Chief Aerodynamicist at Rolls-Royce Ltd. and Professor Renzo Lazzeretti of the Dipartimento di Aerospatiale Ingegnaria, Universita degli Studi di Pisa, both valued friends and encouragers from whose scientific knowledge and personal friendship I have benefitted.

Attempting to write in a popular idiom when my life has been spent in writing scientific treatises was a challenge, and it was the task of Richard Herkes, editor and former publisher, to knock me and my work into shape. Without Richard, this book would be a pile of largely incoherent phrases.